Beginning iOS Cloud and Database Development

Nathan Ooley

Nick Tichawa

Brian Miller

Apress®

Beginning iOS Cloud and Database Development

ISBN-13 (pbk): 978-1-4302-4113-3

ISBN-13 (electronic): 978-1-4302-4114-0

President and Publisher: Paul Manning
Lead Editor: Steve Anglin
Technical Reviewer: Michael Melanson
Editorial Board: Steve Anglin, Mark Beckner, Ewan Buckingham, Gary Cornell, Louise Corrigan, James T. DeWolf, Jonathan Gennick, Jonathan Hassell, Robert Hutchinson, Michelle Lowman, James Markham, Matthew Moodie, Jeff Olson, Jeffrey Pepper, Douglas Pundick, Ben Renow-Clarke, Dominic Shakeshaft, Gwenan Spearing, Matt Wade, Steve Weiss
Coordinating Editor: Anamika Panchoo
Copy Editor: Linda Seifert
Compositor: SPi Global
Indexer: SPi Global
Artist: SPi Global
Cover Designer: Anna Ishchenko

Distributed to the book trade worldwide by Springer Science+Business Media New York, 233 Spring Street, 6th Floor, New York, NY 10013. Phone 1-800-SPRINGER, fax (201) 348-4505, e-mail orders-ny@springer-sbm.com, or visit www.springeronline.com. Apress Media, LLC is a California LLC and the sole member (owner) is Springer Science + Business Media Finance Inc (SSBM Finance Inc). SSBM Finance Inc is a Delaware corporation.

For information on translations, please e-mail rights@apress.com, or visit www.apress.com.

Apress and friends of ED books may be purchased in bulk for academic, corporate, or promotional use. eBook versions and licenses are also available for most titles. For more information, reference our Special Bulk Sales–eBook Licensing web page at www.apress.com/bulk-sales.

Any source code or other supplementary materials referenced by the author in this text is available to readers at www.apress.com. For detailed information about how to locate your book's source code, go to www.apress.com/source-code/.

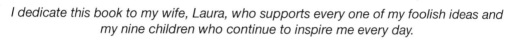

I dedicate this book to my wife, Laura, who supports every one of my foolish ideas and my nine children who continue to inspire me every day.

—Nathan Ooley

Contents at a Glance

Contents

About the Authors

Early in his career, **Nathan Ooley** served on a U.S. battleship utilizing GPS and radio frequency as an Electronic Warfare Tech in the Navy in the late 1980s. He was instantly fascinated with technology working in a battle-ready environment. After the Navy, he landed his first job at small print shop in Minneapolis working with small agencies and print campaigns. He returned to school for graphic design and printing with hopes of pursuing a career in print. After college he worked in printing and marketing for next 12 years.

While working as a project manager for one of the largest direct mail printers, he managed strategic relationships with large advertising agencies for the direct mail campaigns. He continued in print sales for leading direct web printer and secured a $1.2M advertising account with Dish Network. Nathan was recognized as a top sales performer during his work at print and advertising companies in the 1990s.

As the trend to digital publishing became more apparent, his lifelong hobby turned into a calling for the next evolution, commercial level programing in HTML. He is self-taught and continued development as a programmer and further defined his technical path into HTML and data-driven web applications. Early career projects include developing sites with streaming video at low bandwidth in the late 1990s when 256k download speed was fast.

His success grew in web development and consulting during the website boom of the early to mid-2000s. In 2007, when Steve Jobs announced the iPhone SDK, Nathan predicted that a smartphone would be the next evolution of development and focused 100% on mobile development. After two years of independent development, Nathan founded Appmosphere Inc, a full-service mobile application development company. With growth of 200% each year, Appmosphere has developed over 20 business applications and helped several companies incorporate mobile technology into their business. This is where Global Storm POS got its start.

In 2013, Nathan incorporated Global Storm POS as Appmosphere's flagship software and has focused resources and team members on its launch in 2014.

Nick Tichawa is a writer with experience writing in many formats, including technical writing, developing marketing copy, crafting novels and short stories, blogging, and more. He obtained a bachelor's degree in English and Cultural Studies from the University of Minnesota on a full scholarship. Beyond his writing background, he is well-versed in the tech environment. In 2012, he joined the software development firm, Appmosphere Inc., where he has helped manage mobile application production. Comfortable with wireless networking, Nick is CompTIA Network+ certified. He is also a registered as an Apple Mobility Technical Consultant and as such, has helped schools and retail environments deploy mobile devices and wireless networks.

Brian Miller started out as an Electrical and Environmental Systems Mechanic on the KC-135R Aircraft in the United States Air Force. Within his first two years he was supervising and training other airmen on all tasks related to their proficiencies. By year three he was assigned to the Singapore Air Force to train their staff on all tasks required to maintain and repair E&E systems. Brian later became Director of Development and Web Software Engineer at Sound Impressions LLC. One of his major tasks was to create policies and procedures that allowed the company to become dynamically scalable. Re-organizing servers, code management, and process workflow were key to his position and the success of the company. Brian began as a self-taught C and C++ Programmer in 1998. Future languages included HTML, PHP, Java, JavaScript, Objective C, and C#. He is also proficient in database technologies such as MS Access, MSSQL, MySQL, and SQLite. Brian excels at troubleshooting and implementing new technologies. Brian is currently the VP of Software Development with Appmosphere, Inc.

About the Technical Reviewer

Michael Melanson has been developing software professionally for over a decade, mostly with startups and as a consultant. He is a full-stack developer specializing in web services and mobile applications using a variety of technologies. Michael lives with his wife in Ottawa, Canada.

Introduction

We are really excited for the future of cloud development for programmers. There is no question that the majority of applications we will develop over the next few years will have some type of connection to the cloud.

In this book, we cover each of the basic saving methods in detail. We start with creating container objects and change notifications, and then we cover the basics of data connections. We also discuss Key Values, best user practices, and how to get this lightweight data quickly to your applications. Next, we dive in a little deeper and discuss in detail how to add Documents and Core Data.

Building great iCloud applications also takes a vision of what is possible with early technology, such as iCloud and other cloud services. As we develop with new phases of technology we should always reach for what is next out there and develop those technologies further to see if they fit into our vision and style. We investigate new trends in the industry and what the iOS engineers offer developers to take that technology further.

This book hopefully opens up possibilities that you as a developer can look at to get started developing data-driven applications with iCloud and further develop your skills for adding iCloud to your application.

We also cover issues that network connections have when trying to sync your data. Connectivity is always going to be a variable, never a constant. Connectivity is fluid, as mobile users may experience a slow network, a public network, and an LTE network all within the same public area. These variables have an impact on how you design your methods and code architecture. Before you write that first line of code, you learn how to create your user experience wireframe with every scenario in mind. If there is anything we want you to take from this book, it is design and user experience must be considered on the frontend rather than the backend. It's easy to say that Apple has all these situations figured out, but it's important for you as a developer to differentiate your end-user's experience. We will cover some pitfalls and how to avoid them.

iCloud is relatively simple to integrate. You have great APIs built in that are easy to integrate into the workflow. Once you have the essentials covered in this book and develop your first application, you'll be well on your way to understanding what database integration can bring to your application. I hope that you enjoy the step-by-step approach here. This book can help mold your baseline foundation for connecting your local data to iCloud using Key Values, Documents and Core Data.

Let's get started…

Cloud Database Development — The Basics

Just so we can start at the same place, I want to cover a quick overview of database development. Since database development can be a book of its own, understanding it is key, as it is the backbone of the journey that will take place in this book. I won't go too extensively into the topic but want to at least cover the basics for getting us started on the path of developing an iCloud application. I expect people reading this book to be somewhat knowledgeable of databases and how they work. This chapter serves as a refresher on databases and sheds some light on the back-end systems we often take for granted. Remote and cloud databases are still a relatively new subject, especially when relating to how they can be used with mobile applications. Understanding how connections are made and the ways they are being used in the modern world are important when it comes time to think through your application and begin coding. While this book focuses primarily on iCloud development, it's also important to be aware of other database platforms such as Azure and MySQL. Most likely, you won't be able avoid these other platforms for long, and cloud databases are becoming so necessary in today's world, having a general understanding of other systems is crucial.

Anyone who's used a program such as Excel will have some experience with data tables. Having data broken down into characters and fields and realizing how those interact with one another gives us a deeper perspective than the average user receives. Also, many of you reading this will also have experience with some database management system or another, but may not be aware of the many functions and capabilities of these systems. By gaining a better understanding of cloud services, as well as the types of databases, you'll be able gain greater clarity on how users will interact with your database, and how it should be structured. Now let's dig a bit deeper into the cloud.

Explanation of a Remote or Cloud Database

Whether or not you like it, many of the mundane actions you perform throughout the day turn into data that is stored and used by various organizations. Whether using an automated calculator for filling out a form on your iPad or ordering a new book on Amazon, all this data gets compiled and sorted into various databases. As a mobile developer, you will need to consider the architecture of the database you're connecting to and how to access that data remotely.

Businesses store data for primarily financial and legal reasons. Companies and organizations need to collect and store vast amounts of data about their employees' and customers' finances, various habits, and so on. In addition to legal reasons for keeping this information, data can be used to see trends over time, manage inventory, compare with competitors, and so forth. Data allows monitoring and acting on an individual's personal buying habits. The data that is collected is becoming increasingly important as corporations become more global. Companies can capture large amounts of data from all over the world and use it to recognize and act on the trends they see.

This information collected in databases not only needs to be viewed on computer applications, but also has to be accessible on mobile devices. This means data input on a mobile device needs to be continually reconciled with the application server that's hosting the data. An example would be a company that needs to keep track of all their projects and the materials needed to produce those projects. In most cases, there are several devices accessing this data. The database is keeping track of several data sets. For example, an administrator adjusts a data set, which, depending on the variables involved, will adjust other data sets. Because the availability and costs of individual parts to make an end-product are always changing, the administrator can set individual costs, operating costs, and other data that needs to be captured into a working database. They could then potentially see tables, charts, graphs, projection estimates, price suggestions, and so on, all based on this data. This access to the company numbers could be important to a manager. But the information, how it's displayed, and the types of comparisons, graphs, or predictions all depends on the parameters defined when laying out the database. The true value of this data cannot be appropriately valued without making sure that this data is organized and is accessible to the right users. The latter thought, accessibility to the right users, is where the cloud comes in.

A *remote cloud database* is a server that sits on a rack somewhere in the world and is connected to the Internet. It has a server application running and has extra hardware. It is connected to high-speed Internet. So when I talk about data services and about "connecting to the cloud," I am talking about connecting to the server. The critical task of every server is to create a connectable directory that has different types of data stored. The cloud distributes that data quickly. Running a powerful server with the latest hardware has the best capabilities for manipulating, querying, and extracting data and metadata.

Now that we've covered a little bit about cloud databases, let's tie this concept into other kinds of database development.

Types of Database Development

One of the newer cloud services is iCloud from Apple. This book primarily discusses iCloud and the features that iCloud has built into it. Apple has established a very user-friendly system for developers' connections with their service. For example, I mentioned a cloud's ability to quickly distribute data and hardware that is capable of manipulating, querying, and extracting data and metadata. One of iCloud's nicest features is how it handles your file's metadata. This document service makes sure to always push metadata to the cloud ahead of the data that is actually changed in the file. This means that your application is aware of the files that are available to it before the file data has been completely pushed to iCloud or downloaded to a device.

We discuss database development, but more specifically we'll be talking about how that development is best worked into an online and data-driven application. When I talk about applications in this book, I will be primarily speaking of mobile applications. That's not to say that you couldn't develop a desktop or web application to access the database, it's just not something I will be covering in this book.

Database Platforms and Services

I spoke earlier of data management platforms used with businesses. There is a variety of these database management system (DBMS) companies that are available for businesses to work with, including SAP, Oracle, MySQL, and Apple. These management systems need to be defined differently from what resides on the actual databases. Data that is managed is always referred to as "actual data." Many of these companies have very different ways of managing their online database, comprising the "services" part of the DBMSs.

Within a database, raw data alone is not useful. Suppose we did a market research study where we interviewed 50 employees and asked each a series of 25 questions. Once each person has answered the questions, you want to compare the results. Say you want to find all the employees who have become dissatisfied about certain issues. How would you know how to make this comparison?

You have to ask yourself how important each piece of data is before putting filters in the database to decipher it. This helps us structure conclusions based on that data. Some information captured and imported into the database is going to be more important than other information. Not only do you need to decide which pieces of data are included, but also which pieces that are included are the most important, and then structure filters and hierarchies accordingly. This is the key to database management.

With iCloud, the data within your document exists in iCloud until you explicitly request that it be downloaded. Then, once the file is downloaded, iCloud propagates any changes to the document down to your device. This function is another great benefit of iCloud. It is handled this way in order to conserve the storage space on your mobile device. So when you edit a document on your device, the document service only pulls down the individual file that is needed for editing, leaving the rest of it on the server. The application is still aware of these other files because of the metadata that is being persisted across devices. This makes iCloud an efficient data management platform that happens to be perfect for mobile devices, which tend to not have as much storage space as a general computer.

In many ways, iCloud extends beyond what is normally considered a data management platform. Not only does iCloud have a cloud server similar to some of the data management platforms listed previously, but it can update documents other ways as well, such as peer-to-peer.

Characters and Fields

Characters are the basic element of data for the purpose of this book. Non-textual data is also considered data but not in the way I will be describing. For purposes of this book, we will be discussing only textual data. Those characters are the building blocks of the field, which are the building blocks of the record and the table.

A *field* contains an item of data—a character, or group of characters that are related. For example, a grouping of related text characters such as "Erin" makes up a first name in the name field in Figure 1-1.

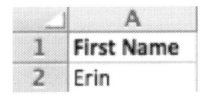

Figure 1-1. Example of a field (First Name) and four characters (Erin)

For each person in our example, we must identify the name, address, city, state, zip code, and telephone number. A field is established for each type of information in the list. The First Name field contains all the letters of the first name. The zip code field holds all the digits of a person's zip code, and so on. In summary, a field may contain an attribute (e.g., employee salary) or the name of an entity (e.g., person, place, or event).

Records and Tables

A *record* is composed of a group of related fields. It contains a collection of attributes related to an entity, such as a person or product. When all gathered, it contains the most important information for you to be accessing.

As shown in Figure 1-2, you have the name, address, zip code, and telephone number of a single individual that would constitute a record. This group of five records becomes a table of the database.

A	B	C	D	E
First Name	Last Name	DOB	Address	Social Security
Erin	Gibb	3/2/54	1201 Westmore Dr	664-20-2345
David	Olsen	3/2/58	33002 Addison Lane	433-41-4978
Jack	Olson	2/3/89	3044 Berrymore Dr	446-59-1102
Mary	Stein	12/21/80	1025 Oregon trail	568-43-2322
Ronald	Gross	1/3/92	22 West 1st Street	460-43-5605

Figure 1-2. An example of 5 records making up a table

The Database File

A *database file* is defined as a collection of related data. A database contains tables with each family of data. A database file may be composed of a complete list of individuals on a mailing list, including their addresses and telephone numbers. Files are frequently categorized by the purpose or application for which they are intended. Some common examples include mailing lists, customer files, inventory files, or document files.

Organizations and individuals use databases to bring independent sources of data together and store them electronically. Thus, a database is composed of related files that are consolidated, organized, and stored together. One collection of related files might pertain to employee information. Another collection of related files might contain the items in the inventory. As you'll see in the next section, the database model consists of multiple tables.

The Relational Database

Relational databases work on the principle that each table has a key field that uniquely identifies each row, and that these key fields can be used to connect one table of data to another. Thus, one table might have a row consisting of a customer account number as the key field along with address and telephone number. The customer account number in this table could be linked to another table of data that also includes customer account number (a key field), but in this case, contains information about product returns, including an item number (another key field). This key field can be linked to another table that contains item numbers and other product information, such as production location, color, quality control person, and other data. Therefore, using this database, customer information can be linked to specific product information.

The relational database has become quite popular for two reasons. First, relational databases can be used with little or no training. Second, database entries can be modified without redefining the entire structure. The downside of using a relational database is that searching for data can take more time than if other methods are used. Figure 1-3 shows an example relational design.

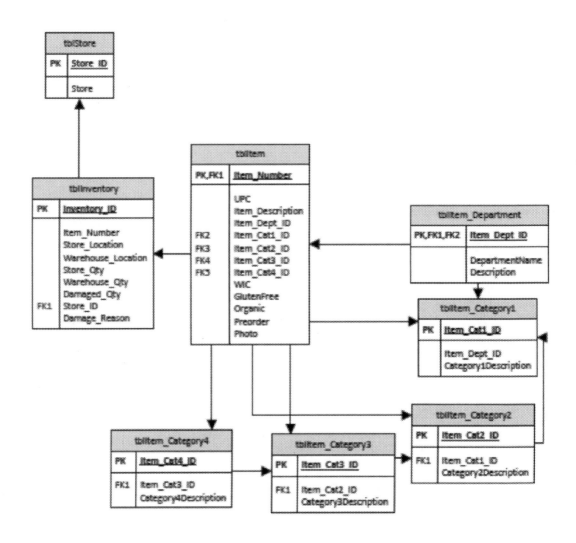

Figure 1-3. An example of a database design wireframe

Organizations and individuals may use many different databases depending on the nature of the work involved. For example, a library database might consist of several related, but separate databases, including book titles and author names, book description, books on order, books checked out, and similar sets of information.

Database Management System

A database management system is used to access and manipulate data in a database. On a basic level, it's a software system that enables users to edit, link, and update files as needs dictate. It is a very customizable approach to managing databases and suits a lot of companies because of that reason alone. With this managed approach, a company would need to spend human resources and consulting time to make sure they have support if the software has a bug. This is another good reason to look at some of the newer systems like iCloud. That being said, while it is not as customizable as the other systems, you can create an application that manages some of this for you. That's why you are reading this book, right?

At the core of every good database is organization. As we saw earlier, in order to track and analyze data effectively, each record requires a unique identifier or a "key." The key must be completely unique to a particular record just as each individual has a unique social security number assigned to them (see Figure 1-4).

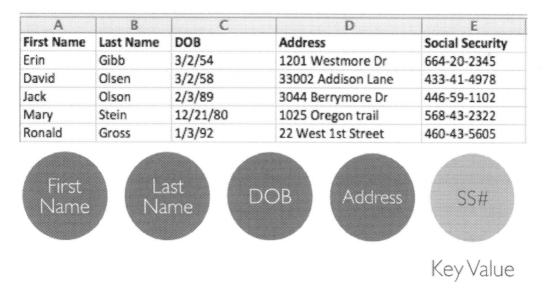

	A	B	C	D	E
	First Name	Last Name	DOB	Address	Social Security
	Erin	Gibb	3/2/54	1201 Westmore Dr	664-20-2345
	David	Olsen	3/2/58	33002 Addison Lane	433-41-4978
	Jack	Olson	2/3/89	3044 Berrymore Dr	446-59-1102
	Mary	Stein	12/21/80	1025 Oregon trail	568-43-2322
	Ronald	Gross	1/3/92	22 West 1st Street	460-43-5605

First Name   Last Name   DOB   Address   SS#

Key Value

Figure 1-4. Each circle in this figure represents a field in the table and the SS# is established as the key value

In fact, social security numbers are often used as keys in large databases. You might think that the name field would be a good choice for a key in a mailing list; however, this would not be a good choice because people might have the same name. A key must be identified or assigned to each record for computerized information processing to function correctly. An existing field may be used if the entries are entirely unique, such as a social security number or telephone number. In most cases, a new field will be developed to hold a key, such as a customer number or product number.

iCloud uses a Ubiquity Identity Token for this function. This is a token that is provided to you by the iCloud Storage API, and it references a particular user on a device within your app. This means that if you are signed in to multiple devices, the Ubiquity Token is different for each device. You can use the Ubiquity Identity Token to first confirm that the user has iCloud set up for their account. It can also be used to determine whether a different user is now using your app on the same device.

Multiple Sources

A database is more useful if there is little redundancy between the files it contains. In other words, it would be inefficient and a waste of human and computer resources to have the same information repeated over and over again in different files. Some companies maintain databases with very similar information. Sometimes there are good reasons for this; e.g. for security purposes. However, it's simply more costly to maintain accurate information in multiple locations. In addition, there would also be a need to resolve discrepancies occurring between the same information in multiple files.

iCloud has an automatic conflict resolution. This means that if you edit the same file on two different devices at the same time iCloud will see that these edits are in conflict. It will resolve the conflict automatically by selecting what it believes is the most up to date file. However, you are also notified of this conflict. The iCloud Storage API also lets you traverse through file versions and resolve the conflict manually if needed.

One of the beauties of cloud databases is linking together data from multiple sources to accomplish a specific task. This can be accomplished on mobile devices, and users can interact with the cloud like they have never done before. Writing applications that utilize these services will become more of the norm going forward in a connected world. Users demand the need to access their data and share with others. Now many users need to have the same experience on their tablet or phone and have confidence that their data is secure and accessible.

The Advantages of a Cloud Database Management System

One of the principle advantages of a cloud management system is that the same information can be made available to different users.

The data in the cloud is more concise because, as a general rule, the information in it appears just once. This reduces data redundancy, or in other words, the need to repeat the same data over and over again. Minimizing redundancy can therefore significantly reduce the cost of storing information on hard drives and other storage devices. In contrast, data fields are commonly repeated in multiple files when a file management system is used.

Accurate, consistent, and up-to-date data is a sign of data integrity. Cloud database management systems maintain data integrity because updates and changes to the data only have to be made in one place. The chances of making a mistake are much higher if you are required to change the same data in several different places than if you only have to make the change in one place.

When using a cloud database management system, file formats and system programs are standardized. This makes the data files easier to maintain because the same rules and guidelines apply across all types of data. The level of consistency across files and programs also makes it easier to manage data when multiple programmers are involved and are working on the same project.

Data is easier to access and manipulate with a cloud solution than without one. As we are usually not far from Wi-Fi and cellular LTE networks, we have the ability to be online at almost all times. In most cases, cloud services also reduce the reliance of individual users on computer specialists to meet their data needs.

As stated earlier, cloud database management services allow multiple users to access the same data resources. This capability is generally viewed as a benefit, but there are potential risks for the organization. Some sources of information should be protected or secured and only viewed by select individuals. Through the use of passwords and transport security, database management systems can be used to restrict data access to only those who are authorized to see it.

The Disadvantages of a Cloud Database Management System

There are two major downsides to using cloud database management systems. One of these is cost, and the other is threat to data security.

Implementing a cloud database management system can be expensive and time-consuming, especially in large organizations. Training requirements alone can be quite costly. This is where I believe application developers like us can create unique experiences for the user to limit this learning curve.

Even with the best safeguards in place, it may be possible for some unauthorized users to access your database. In general, database access is an all or nothing proposition. Once an unauthorized user gets into your database, he has access to all the files, not just a few. Depending on the nature of the data involved, these breaches in security can also pose a threat to individual privacy. Steps should always be taken to regularly make backup copies of the database files and store them because of the possibility of fires and natural disasters that might destroy the system. This is another reason to use a company such as Apple or Microsoft to manage these services so you can concentrate on developing great applications and leave the management of the data to someone else.

Summary

This book is going to really need to be tied in to how iCloud comes out of the box and serves three main features: consumer experience, backup, and availability.

The consumer is very used to having a good experience. By this I mean not replying to several alerts and notifications that are just annoying for most. iCloud doesn't have to ask for passwords, it stores them automatically. This happens in the background, so it is never an issue for the user.

Second, out of the box, we want to make sure that the backup of the data is always available and done automatically because most users don't have that capability or know where to back up the data. iCloud is a seamless integration with backups of user data.

Third,—the last and most important thing—whether it's on my iPad at a meeting, my iPhone on the way home in my car, or later on my laptop, iCloud makes it easy for me to only have the music and videos that I want at any given time. I can download the music and videos from the cloud. This is a data-driven application. When you're creating your application you want to always make sure that you can access that database with all iOS and OS devices. You can manipulate your data on your devices and let iCloud manipulate, store, and compare the data on a server, not your mobile application.

Chapter 2

Introduction to the Cloud

In this chapter, I talk about dynamic data services, specifically iCloud's ability to automatically sync documents across devices, giving users a simple, streamlined, and seamless experience. Because iCloud is simply a server performing a web service, it is certainly possible to have devices continually sync with the cloud using a web service and a SQL database. However, this is much more complicated than in iCloud, as iCloud has all these features built directly in to it, right out of the box. When developing apps natively for iOS, it requires much undue time and effort to work outside the system that has been set up for you. That being said, if an app is not being developed natively, and is instead a hybrid app that contains native and web content, iCloud may no longer be an option. A database such as Azure SQL Database or MySQL may be necessary. Assuming you will be coding natively, this chapter focuses on iCloud and has you syncing documents promptly.

> **Note**   The documents I talk about in this chapter should be thought of as captured, compiled data and include things such as set images and graphics. This is unlike Core Data, which can be thought of as raw, uncompiled data. I will cover Core Data in a later chapter.

The Movement to the Cloud

The cloud is a way for us to move data off our local storage system. What was once a novel practice is now becoming common. Having your data stored outside your building or company walls allows for more connection services, as well as some specialized services. For example, iCloud and certain other cloud services enable developers to ensure that once all the data is saved and sustained, it is the same across all devices. One of the best features of iCloud is the simplicity of adding devices and syncing across them.

We live in the second decade of the 21st-century. It feels appropriate that we have reached our capacity for making bigger hard drives and computers. They are becoming less and less common. Instead, companies such as Amazon have started to create server farms where it can keep adding servers or clouds, as companies require their services. At the same time, mobile devices are becoming faster, cheaper, and smaller. Consumption from these devices is increasing dramatically with more and more data being sent across all our mobile devices or desktops daily. Especially within businesses, this is becoming more critical every day. The trend appears to be moving toward online and cloud services because it makes sense with the world in which we now live. We are trying to make cheaper, faster, smaller devices that don't hold a lot of data, but still have an enormous capacity for data consumption and processes that are much faster than the processors that we carry around in our pockets. Even our latest smartphone is faster than a desktop computer from 10 years ago. It has become more and more evident that we need services that store large amounts of data but also give us access to it quickly.

Table 2-1 shows the top ten applications and the amount of usage compared to others. Five of the ten are data-driven applications. The other five are applications for downloading from these and other sites.

Table 2-1. Mobile streaming data comparison (Source: Sandvine Network Demographics)

	Upstream		Downstream		Aggregate	
Rank	Application	Share	Application	Share	Application	Share
1	Facebook	15.43%	YouTube	30.97%	YouTube	28.03%
2	HTTP	13.60%	HTTP	14.37%	HTTP	14.28%
3	SSL	13.26%	SSL	8.92%	SSL	9.49%
4	YouTube	7.91%	MPEG	8.90%	Facebook	7.95%
5	Google Talk	2.23%	Facebook	6.83%	MPEG	7.93%
6	MPEG	1.92%	Pandora Radio	5.15%	Pandora Radio	4.74%
7	Pandora Radio	1.90%	Google Play	3.27%	Google Play	2.96%
8	Skype	1.56%	Netflix	2.69%	Netflix	2.42%
9	SMTP	1.52%	iTunes	1.46%	iTunes	1.34%
10	Yahoo! Mail	1.49%	Flash Video	1.18%	Flash Video	1.05%
	Top 10	60.82%	Top 10	83.74%	Top 10	80.19%

In Table 2-2, you see the trend is the same for all fixed access or desktop users.

Table 2-2. *Fixed access data streaming comparison (Source: Sandvine Network Demographics)*

	Upstream		Downstream		Aggregate	
Rank	Application	Share	Application	Share	Application	Share
1	BitTorrent	36.8%	Netflix	33.0%	Netflix	28.8%
2	HTTP	9.83%	YouTube	14.8%	YouTube	13.1%
3	Skype	4.76%	HTTP	12.0%	HTTP	11.7%
4	Netflix	4.51%	BitTorrent	5.89%	BitTorrent	10.3%
5	SSL	3.73%	iTunes	3.92%	iTunes	3.43%
6	YouTube	2.70%	MPEG	2.22%	SSL	2.23%
7	PPStream	1.65%	Flash Video	2.21%	MPEG	2.05%
8	Facebook	1.62%	SSL	1.97%	Flash Video	2.01%
9	Apple PhotoStream	1.46%	Amazon Video	1.75%	Facebook	1.50%
10	Dropbox	1.17%	Facebook	1.48%	RTMP	1.41%
	Top 10	68.24%	Top 10	79.01%	Top 10	76.54%

Why Develop an App with the Cloud?

Storing your company data on the cloud can make good business sense. If your application requires you to field service station calls while out in the field and you need to access your data remotely, having it in the cloud will be of great help.

We always have to think about who is going to be using this data and how are they going to be using it. So, if the field agent is using a pricing application that you have developed, and all that information is stored within the application, if those products change prices, they won't be able to be updated correctly from a server. There's no way for you to protect your data when it isn't downloaded from a server. If the application were connected to the cloud, simple protocols would be in place so that if Joe the salesman had your application and all of a sudden he decided to go to different company or decided to use your prices, and you felt like that was the end of his job that day, you can, within a short amount of time, disable his application. Joe would have the most recent data but it wouldn't be updatable with his security level taken away, and with most of the data still on the cloud hidden from him.

If you're dependent on the call data within that application, and if it's critical that user experience be robust, then maybe the cloud is not the correct server platform. But let's just say you have an application that has multiple platforms. This would be a no-brainer. The cloud allows the application on all the platforms to have one center point of data rather than managing multiple data centers. This makes pragmatic sense when you're programming for mobile applications, especially when they are cross-platform.

Now that we've decided that it's time to develop a cloud application or data in the cloud, the first question that you have to ask is how do you want to track different types of data. You want to have your variables already decided in a way that makes sense with best business practices.

Designing for the cloud takes an understanding, from an iCloud standpoint, of how it synchronizes data across devices. So, when you're working with your JSON, you have a good understanding of what it takes to read data from a dedicated source, or know how to access that data in your application and display the data once you receive it. This requires a clear understanding that your local application is highly dependent on network connectivity. You also need to consider if there needs to be an offline mode and how that impacts your application. If offline is a consideration, then you need to set up a protocol for syncing when offline. You want to show this in the UI. I discuss caching and taking data from the cloud and accessing it later. In programmer's terms, this is the API (Application Programming Interface).

For the most part, users want to access to data, and if that data changes, they want to know immediately through a push notification or an update to the application. All you need to do is make sure that you have an understanding of how your application will handle the data and what data will be driving the majority of the app after it has been downloaded. Think about this when you're designing your core application: the data from the cloud is going to be a large part of it and having access to the updated data or showing your users that there is other data available will be of utmost importance. Once users can look at the application, they should see the data on the cloud versus the local data. It is very important for your user to know they are looking at the right data, as this service is meant to have a seamless interface and a user experience that doesn't do a lot of work in front of the user. Users want to know that the work is going on behind-the-scenes and that they have the most up-to-date content without having to check and be sure.

What Are iCloud's Key Offerings?

Apple announced its iCloud service in 2011 with the advent of iOS 5. In the most basic terms, iCloud is simply an open directory on Apple servers that can connect with applications. While Apple has used its experience in marketing to give their product an interesting name, in actuality it is simply a box performing "server-side scripting" that would take an expert developer a lot of time to set up.

iCloud provides solutions for the problems of both digital storage and file sharing between devices. It allows digital content to be continuously updated and synced on all of the user's devices without making the user think about it. iCloud is designed to enhance Apple applications and improve the user's experience by using Apple's servers to sync files and data. Once a user's app has the necessary connections to work with iCloud, it does all the hard work for them. In virtually real time it syncs all the data, so there is no more worrying about whether data has been copied to each of a user's devices—it has. iCloud has many other functions, such as storing several types of data.

When iCloud is enabled on an app on a device, any update made to that application is automatically sent out to iCloud, and any time any other changes come in from any other device, iCloud sees the updated file and makes sure that the same applications on the user's other linked devices also receive the updated file. Figure 2-1 shows this concept.

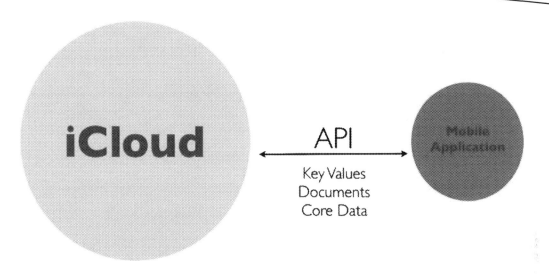

Figure 2-1. *The three core functions of the iCloud API*

When the user makes alterations to a document on his device, iCloud notices each of the changes and makes updates to the documents that have not yet been changed on other devices. iCloud only sends out the differences in the document, which then become versions of the original. There is virtually no labor necessary on the part of the user. The application handles the issue of sending the files up to iCloud. This process actually involves breaking down the document into several smaller pieces of data, called "chunks" or "pieces," and then pinpointing the data that has been changed. These chunks are then sent to all the devices connected the user's Apple ID. This then becomes version two of the document.

The place where you store files that you want to sync to iCloud is called the Ubiquity Container. The Ubiquity Container serves as a master file and is designated as the vehicle that passes your documented data between your devices and iCloud (see Figure 2-2).

Figure 2-2. iCloud reads the Ubiquity Container to check for changes

Designing for iCloud

This efficient process of only sending chunks of data keeps us from having to send megabytes or even gigabytes of data back and forth to iCloud. In addition to these chunks, files in your applications also have a lot of associated information, such as name, modification date, size, file type, and so on. This metadata is pushed to iCloud as well.

Most apps also aggressively push all this metadata to iCloud, so that even before a file is finished uploading, the name, modification date, and so on, are identifiable in iCloud. This makes for a better user experience, because even though the file may not be opened immediately, it will still show the data as a placeholder on the screen.

iOS and Mac OS iCloud

There is a significant difference between how OS X and iOS handle file downloads. Any files that are stored on OS X are downloaded aggressively from the iCloud to the Mac. This is because iCloud knows that a Mac has more storage capacity than your iOS device. With iOS devices, applications know all the files that are available in iCloud, but the application will only ask for specific files to be brought down to the device. This saves a significant amount of storage on the device and allows for faster download speeds.

iCloud also can copy files directly between two devices, or between an iMac and iPad, provided they are on the same network. Taking a file and sending it up to iCloud and then waiting for it to download back to your iPad may seem like a long way to go if the devices are on the same network, but iCloud recognizes this and actually sends the data peer to peer over the network.

iCloud storage is focused on a silent user experience when moving data between devices. iCloud notifies the application of file changes any time a device receives new content that is coming from the server. This symbiotic update works even if your application is not running. Executed by the operating system, all these functions still work properly. It makes the task of development easier, as the focus can remain in the sandbox of the application.

The goal of iCloud application development is to create a fundamental way to distribute data and enhance the user's experience. Users want to be able to pick up any of their devices and simply have the data and settings from their applications available to them.

A great example of iCloud technology is the Photo Stream in Apple's iPhoto app. Photo Stream enables users to look at their pictures as well as upload their most recently taken photos to their iCloud account. Photos are uploaded immediately to the cloud without any action necessary on the part of the user, allowing for easy collaboration between users sharing the Photo Stream. Users can then view these recently uploaded images through a number of applications such as iTunes, iPhoto, or another Apple app such as Keynote. iPhoto comes with iCloud built in and is a great app for utilizing iCloud, as it offers users a wide range of possibilities such as posting photos to their Apple TV or to the screensaver on their Mac.

It is important to remember that the primary benefit of Photo Stream or any other iCloud application is that it takes no conscious effort on the part of the user. Yes, iCloud also backs up files, but ease and convenience are the driving forces here. Once a user takes a photo on their iPhone, Photo Stream makes it instantly available to them in iPhoto. When figuring out ways to integrate applications into iCloud, remember that ease and simplicity for the user come first.

iCloud, along with other cloud services can be incredibly useful to your app, and depending on the app's intended functionality, you may need to integrate. Cloud services have exploded in popularity in only a couple years, and their integration may soon become a necessity for most mobile software.

What Are the Expectations of Knowledge for Programming?

I expect you to have a basic understanding of Objective-C if not advanced programming capabilities and experience with Objective-C.

What you really want to have is experience with data connections and an understanding of how the capabilities of mobile devices play a part in your programming so that you can give users the best experience possible. You should be familiar with Xcode and have some exposure to Xcode 5. Your overall understanding of mobile application programming and working with iCloud, whether on the desktop or in a mobile application, needs to be deeper than just the basics. You should have, at a minimum, a baseline knowledge of APIs and have experience working with DB connections, as well as experience in writing classes to connect to those APIs.

Summary

In this chapter, we took a look at cloud services. Because of the recent advances in smaller, more efficient devices, there has been a push to move data to cloud service platforms. The data doesn't need to be stored locally, and many of the complex calculations can actually be performed on the server before being sent to the device, which allows for a simple, streamlined experience. A cloud database allows for these devices to not only quickly pull data from the server, but also for swift syncing between multiple devices, with the cloud database as the central hub. This also lets programs running on multiple platforms be synced via one central location. A cloud solution may not be the best in every situation, but in today's modern, synchronized, and global world, it has become a necessity in many instances.

We also discussed several aspects of cloud services in this chapter, such as how APIs handle the movement of key values, documents, and Core Data. With iCloud specifically, we learned about the efficient process of breaking the data into chunks, which are then sent between iCloud and a user's devices to optimize the amount of data that is sent. We talked about the Ubiquity Container, which serves as the master file and vehicle that passes your document data between iCloud and your devices. And finally, we discussed how iCloud handles data exchange between OS X and iOS, and what programming knowledge you should reasonably be expected to have before moving forward. In the next chapter, we'll be discussing more examples of applications that have benefited from different cloud databases.

Chapter 3

Applications for the Cloud

In this chapter we discuss the options and reasons for developing an application in the cloud. We look exclusively at an application system and why there are benefits to building applications for the cloud. Data-driven applications have several options and personal preference may prevail in your decision to choose one over the other. All the options may work for you, but some cloud services have different options. MySQL accounts for the majority of cloud development. Whether you are looking for the cloud to sync data, back up, or just read cloud data for your application, cloud services are becoming more popular to develop.

Case Study of Storm: A Data-Driven, Cloud-Based Solution

Storm POS™ offers all the integrated mobile solutions a store in the food service, hospitality, or retail industry might need. It helps large retail establishments save time and money over traditional POS systems, while retaining the ability to customize the entire system around their specific brand.

Mobility and streamlined integration is where the retail and service industries are heading. Large retail establishments are beginning to change the way typical business is performed, and expect their technology to keep pace with an increasingly smart and mobile world. Storm POS mobile software products and services provide businesses a chance to get ahead of the competition by supplying them with sleek, efficient, and intuitive mobile tools, some of which are shown in Figure 3-1.

19

Figure 3-1. You can use multiple devices to access the cloud using Storm POS

Case Study of iCloud: Storm Manager App

Working alongside the point-of-sale system is the Storm Manager app. Optimized for tablets, the Manager app works as an analytics tool with the ability to view employee, inventory, and sales analytics, and create actionable reports. This app works in tandem with the point-of-sale, not only behind the scenes, but directly, by allowing cashiers to alert managers of various issues at the register in a discreet and efficient manner. So when a cashier needs change, an item is not on file, or an item needs to be voided, the manager's tablet can be alerted for swift action.

If the Point-of-Sale app is the featured app of the Storm solution, the Manager app is the central hub of the operation, pulling large amounts of data and metrics from the database for many uses. The Manager app generates reports from everything relating to sales, ads, and freight prices to employee productivity and tardiness. It sends and receives alerts from the Stock and POS apps. The Manager app creates and adjusts prices, sets inventory, and helps create ads for print. To be able to perform all these functions, extensive work needs to be performed on the database. It is a large app, requiring complex algorithms and swift communication to take place on the cloud server.

Managers and administrators at the store are going to be working on multiple devices, often at the same time. After they use a device they may switch to another device once they get home, or they may need to look at a report on a different device. As the managers in this ecosystem access and save documents and key data from the iPad, it is uploaded to the cloud, where it can then be accessed and updated on the iPhone. The reporting data from the device is then backed up on iCloud where it can be accessed from different devices from the same manager.

We chose iCloud for this solution because of its simplicity and ease of use. We could've looked at other cross-platform or MySQL databases, but when not looking at data on different devices, and exclusively in the iOS atmosphere, we felt iCloud was the best solution.

When a manager looks at a report, such as a grocery aisle report of sales over the past seven months, he can easily close that application, put his iPad back on the charger and then save the data. Once he gets home he can pick up his iPhone and all that data is available to him. Once the app syncs with the iCloud, the documents that were created for the data were automatically saved by him and categorized based on their user account.

Case Study of Azure: Grocery Store Customer Application

We can develop apps specifically for the use of customers. These apps have the ability to integrate directly with the Storm applications. Options include allowing customers to make shopping lists of items in the database, or when used in tandem with the Stock app, allowing them to preorder specific items so that stock employees can have them ready when customers arrive at the store.

As this book is being written, we are about 8 to 12 months into the cycle of an Azure SQL database and what that service offers. We talked about some possible scenarios, but one real-life scenario takes place in the Customer app in our grocery store suite of apps. The primary reason we chose to use this database is because the Customer app needs to be cross-platform. It's not possible for the grocery store to reach everyone who they want without a cross-platform app. The app needs to support not only Android and iOS, but Windows 8 as well. This is a spot where Azure has a clear advantage over iCloud's SQL database and a standard MySQL database.

We created a customer application that has backend database connections. In this customer application we feel it would be good to have a customer loyalty program. We want to keep track of the user interactions with the database and push notifications to regular users to send them special offers or other information based on their user's information within the database. If we know a user suddenly begins adding baby formula to her grocery list, perhaps we try to find a way to send her an ad for diapers her next time in.

There will be many other functions of this customer application, many of which will require restricted access to the grocery store's data. The customer can make lists of items specific to her store, and she can even preorder small, select orders and have them ready for pickup. This means that when the Manager app updates the database, deciding which items are available for a pickup order (maybe one night it's the ingredients for a spaghetti dinner), this information is displayed on the Customer app. Once the user decides she wants the spaghetti dinner, and she creates an order for pickup, that information is then pushed to a new table in the database. The Stock app is then on the lookout for that new table to be updated in the database. When the app sees that a change has occurred, it pulls down that data, allowing the employee to gather the ingredients and have them ready for the customer when she pulls up.

Because we have three platforms to cover with the Customer app, iCloud is not going to work, but MySQL is another option, as is Backend as a Service offering such as Firebase, or another SQL store such as PostgreSQL. Writing an API to connect to these mobile services from each one of the devices is certainly manageable. Currently, we're using MySQL in this scenario for users to access the database from the customer application. We will be moving into it as your database because of the ease of service and the tracking capabilities and the fact that it has built-in reporting.

Microsoft has taken a look at the back side of the API connections and really gave developers a great opportunity to manage the services closely. When we talk about connections or concurrent connections, we're talking about APIs. These may need to be adjusted from time to time to allow for greater traffic or increased growth from what is, in essence, the building of your business.

Case Study of MySQL: Storm Point of Sale Application

The Storm POS system features a sleek and intuitive design and extensive functionality developed for mobile tablets. Sure to impress customers at checkout, the tablet can be paired with great peripheral hardware solutions such as receipt printers and cash drawers, or may be integrated with existing hardware. It can also be customized to a company's brand and image, creating a piece of software unique to its establishment. The basic Storm solution gives the POS software the functionality to connect to a database, scanner, receipt printer, cash drawer, credit card processor, and Manager app, with the option to add connectivity to several other devices and peripherals.

With the grocery store database, we create a database on the cloud so that the Manager app can access that data, as well as the POS application. The POS is the brains of the transactions. The Manager app is the brains of the modifications and reports. The software is working to perform its functions and update inventory while the Stock app is pulling inventory. The database Manager app has to read endpoints to that data in the cloud. All three applications are essentially reading and writing from the same database.

Once the applications are online and accessing the database API in real time, we write SQL statements to supply the data for subsequent calls from that connection. We also want to make sure that we are connecting and addressing that data based on the cache set up to allow for smooth user experiences. Because this application is mission critical, we never want to lose data, even if we lose a connection.

With the SQL Server we can accomplish a lot more, especially when using very robust data streams and a strong GUI that's doing business. Simply saving key-value data wouldn't be the most straightforward or quickest way to read/write but because we are connecting with the database on the devices connected, it stores a version of the database so that it is actually utilizing some of the database functions internally. We cache the data for an upload later, depending on the connection speeds of the location. This is so the app can operate online as well as offline. The data is still coming from the server on initialization. We mentioned this before, but we are actually going to use iCloud with the Manager app, but the POS application is server driven and uses a MySQL database.

Chapter 4

Basic Setup of iCloud and Key-Value Storage

In this chapter you will learn the fundamentals of adding iCloud to your application. We discuss the most basic type of storage, the Key-Value Store, but first we walk through provisioning and entitlements.

App IDs, Provisioning, and Entitlements

An *App ID* is the identifier used for your app. This ID is solely unique to your app and cannot be used by anyone else.

By default, an iOS device can run apps from the app store and apps that are included with the OS. *Provisioning* is the process that enables your device to run your app. Provisioning also grants your app iCloud support.

Entitlements are a simple version of access control for your app. When your app is compiled and run, the entitlement is included in the code signature. When your app attempts to access the iCloud service, entitlement allows or disallows access based on the code signature.

Now let's discuss these in more detail before we set them up.

App IDs

As mentioned previously, your App ID is a unique identifier. Once this ID is created, it cannot be changed. There are two parts of an App ID:

- **App ID Prefix:** This is created by Apple when you create your developer account. The Apple ID prefix never changes.

- **App ID Suffix:** It is recommended that this be a reverse-domain style string. An example would be com.domainname.appname.

There are two other pieces of information you need to provide when creating an App ID: the App ID Description and App Services. The App ID Description is a name that you use inside the developer portal and is not seen by anyone else. As for App Services, we will only be concerned with iCloud.

Provisioning

A provisioning profile defines your set of devices. It contains a list of identifiers for all your devices, defines your developer certificate, and grants iCloud support via the App ID. This profile tells the operating system to trust the app that you are developing.

Provisioning profiles are separated into two categories: development and distribution. *Development profiles* are used when you first develop an app locally. The devices that you build and test on are all physically with you. Distribution profiles are used when you deploy your app for testing or submit it to the App Store. We will only be concerned about development profiles in this book.

Entitlements

Entitlements are an important piece of the iOS Security Framework. By enabling entitlements, you are causing the entitlement to be included in the code signature of the app. This is why it is important to always remember to enable the iCloud entitlement for an iCloud app. If you don't, you will not be able to access the iCloud service.

There are two entitlements when dealing with iCloud:

- `com.apple.developer.ubiquity-kvstore-identifier`: This is the entitlement that you set when enabling the Key-Value Store.

- `com.apple.developer.ubiquity-container-identifiers`: This is the entitlement that you set when you are enabling Document Storage.

> **Note**   Document Storage encompasses three different areas: the storage of UIDocuments, Packages, and CoreData.

Setting Up Your App ID and Provisioning Profile

Let's create our App ID and provisioning profile on the Apple Developer website. This sets the stage for opening up Xcode and setting up our new project.

1. Log in to your developer account at `http://developer.apple.com`.

2. Click the iOS Dev Center link.

3. On the right side, click Certificates, Identifiers & Profiles. Select the section as shown in Figure 4-1.

Figure 4-1. The area to accessed by the developer to create Certificates, Identifiers, and Profiles

4.   Under the iOS Apps column, click Identifiers.

5.   App IDs should already be selected. If not, click App IDs.

6.   Click the plus button in the top right to create a new App ID.

7.   Under App ID Description, type **iCloudTestApp** for the Name.

8.   Under App ID Suffix, type **com.*creative-company-name*.icloudtestapp** for Bundle ID.

9.   Under App Services, be sure that "iCloud" is checked. See Figure 4-2.

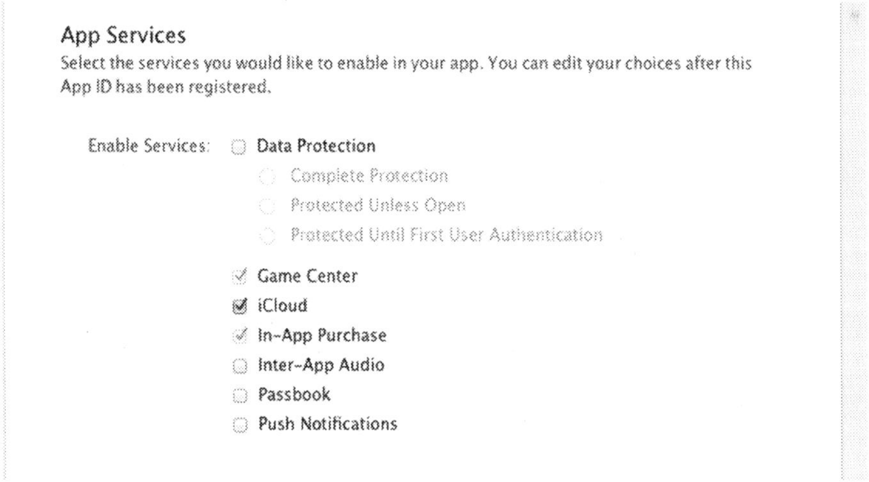

App Services

Select the services you would like to enable in your app. You can edit your choices after this App ID has been registered.

Enable Services: ☐ Data Protection

⬡ Complete Protection

⬡ Protected Unless Open

⬡ Protected Until First User Authentication

☑ Game Center

☑ iCloud

☑ In-App Purchase

☐ Inter-App Audio

☐ Passbook

☐ Push Notifications

Figure 4-2. Apple application services screen

10.   Click Continue at the bottom of the screen.

11.   Confirm the information you entered is correct and click Submit to create the App ID. You can select the ID and then verify that everything is correct on the App services screen. See Figure 4-3 for comparison.

12.   Click Done.

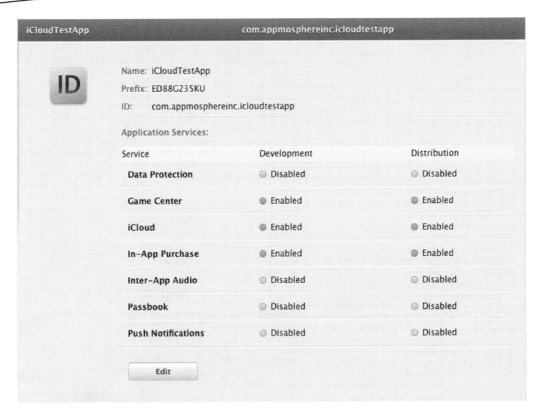

Figure 4-3. Overall services screen

Creating Your Development Provisioning Profile

Now it's time to create a development provisioning profile:

1. Under Provisioning Profiles, click Development. Click the plus button in the top right to create a new provisioning profile.

2. Click the radio button for iOS App Development and click Continue. See Figure 4-4.

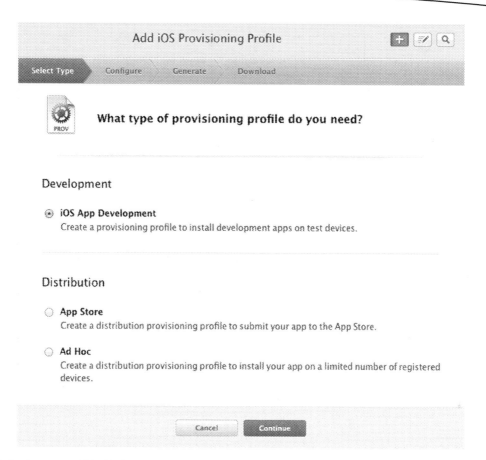

Figure 4-4. *Deployment and Distribution screen for a type of provisioning profile*

3. Select your App ID from the drop-down menu as shown in Figure 4-5. This should be "iCloudTestApp." And click Continue.

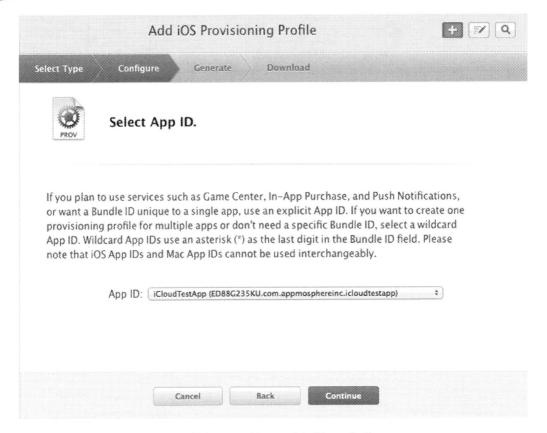

Figure 4-5. Select the development team to which you want to associate this application

4. Select your development certificate. This is most likely your name and click Continue.

5. Put a check mark by your development device and click Continue. See Figure 4-6.

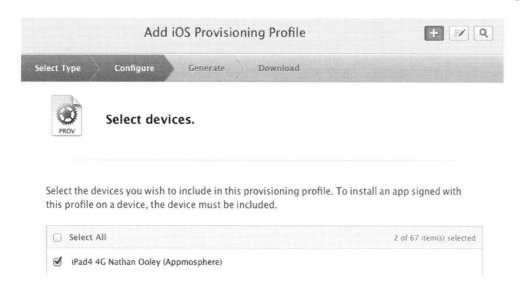

Figure 4-6. Select the device you want to include

6. Type **DeviCloudTestApp** for Profile Name and click Generate. See Figure 4-7.

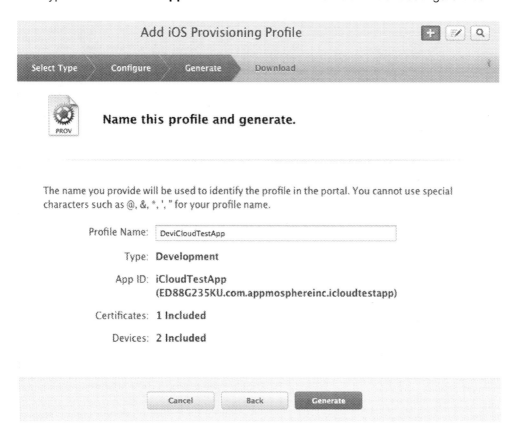

Figure 4-7. Name the profile

> **Note** I find it easier to identify profiles by using the type and the app name together. I normally use Dev, AdHoc, or AppStore, depending on the profile type.

7. Click Done.

Setting Up Your Project in Xcode

You should have a copy of Xcode version 5.0 installed. If you don't, you can download it from the App Store for free. Just search for Xcode or it can usually be found in the Top Free apps list due to its popularity. Now let's create our new project.

1. Create the project in Xcode. Launch Xcode and click the Create a New Xcode Project button on the left. Select Utility Application and click Next as seen in Figure 4-8.

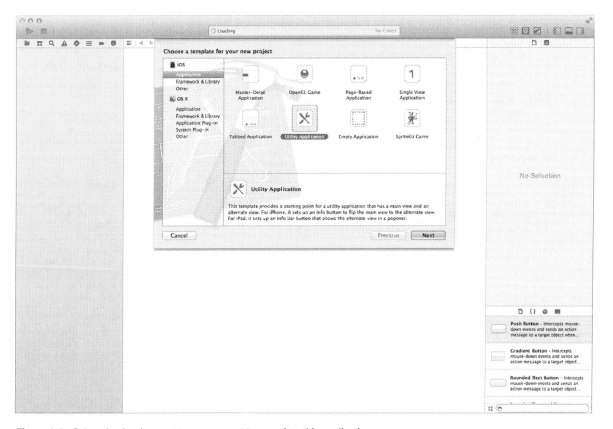

Figure 4-8. Select the development team you want to associate this application

2. For Product Name, type **iCloudTestApp**. You can leave Class Prefix blank.

3. Select iPhone and be sure Use Core Data is checked.

4. As you see in Figure 4-9, this generates some boilerplate set-up and code that we will use in the later chapters. Click Next.

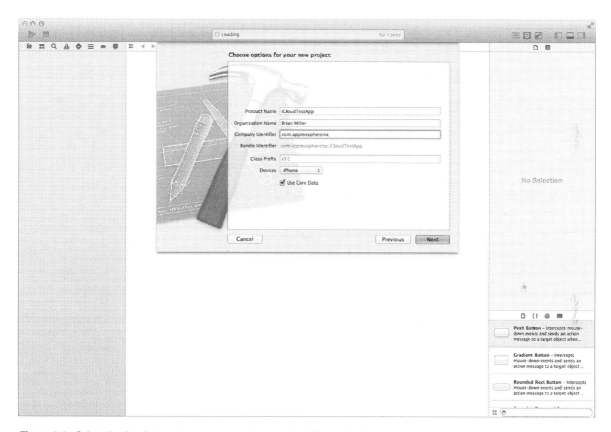

Figure 4-9. *Select the development team you want to associate this application*

5. In the Finder dialog, select the location you want to save your project (as shown in Figure 4-10) and then click Create.

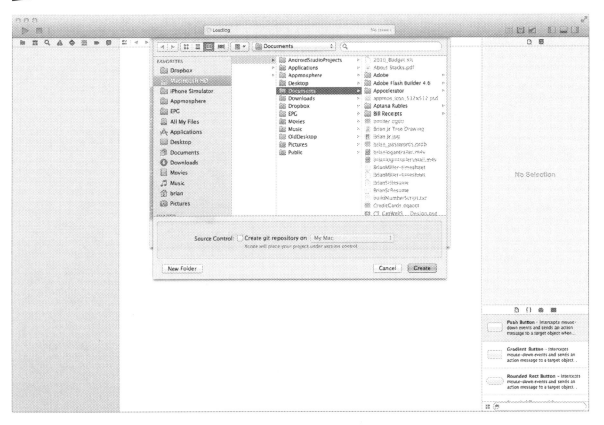

Figure 4-10. Choose where to save your project

Configuring Your Project with iCloud Support

Now that you have a project, let's configure it:

1. Select the project navigator by clicking the Folder icon in the Navigator pane.

2. Click the project iCloudTestApp in the project navigator. Make sure the target selected is the iCloudTestAppTarget in the center pane, as shown in Figure 4-11.

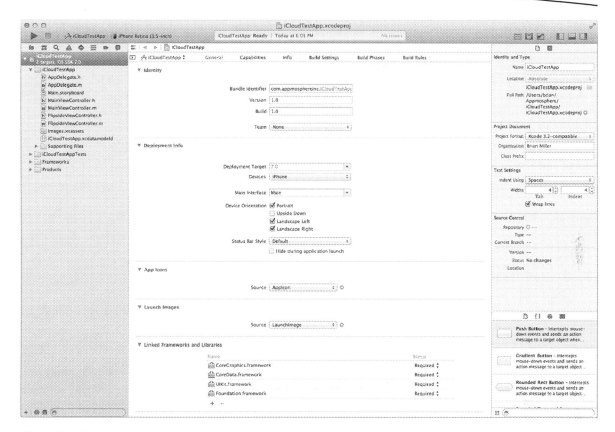

Figure 4-11. Xcode basic parameters setup

Note   You can expand the project and targets list by clicking the expand icon in the top left of the Editor pane.

3. Click the Capabilities tab in the Editor pane and click On, as shown in Figure 4-12.

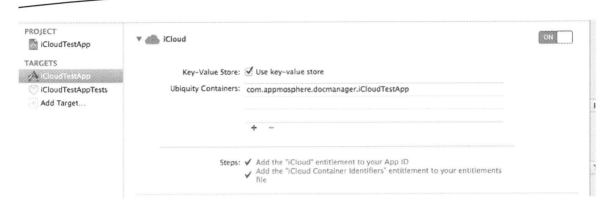

Figure 4-12. *Turn on iCloud Service and confirm Ubiquity Container(s)*

4. In the prompt displayed, select your developer account and click Choose. Check the box for Key-Value Store as shown on Figure 4-13.

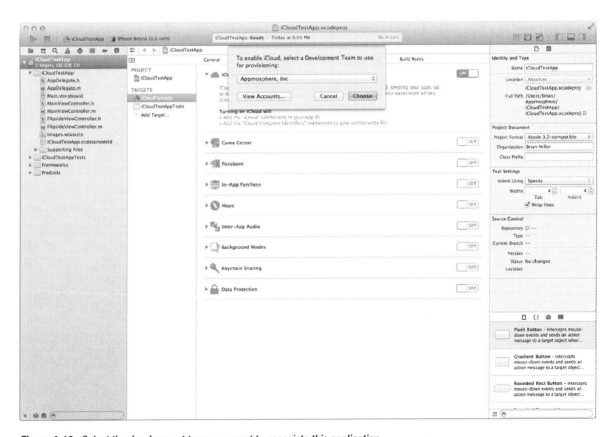

Figure 4-13. *Select the development team you want to associate this application*

Building the Foundation of the App

We will create a simple app that displays a welcome message on the main screen. Inside the Utility Screen there are text fields the user can edit and save. The fields will be saved in the user defaults for the app as well as iCloud. Let's start by building the app without iCloud support.

Organization and Preliminary Setup

In this app we access some methods from the Application Delegate. We create a Define Directive in the precompiled headers file to make this process easier to use later. This is something done in all the apps built and using a shorthand method helps move things along faster.

1. Rename the AppDelegate.h and AppDelegate.m file to CTAppDelegate.h and CTAppDelegate.m, respectively. You can do this by selecting the file in the Project Navigator and then selecting it again.

2. Now let's select the CTAppDelegate.h file and change the comment on line 2 from AppDelegate.h to CTAppDelegate.h.

3. We also want to change the class name on line 11 from AppDelegate to CTAppDelegate.

    ```
    #import <UIKit/UIKit.h>
    @interface CTAppDelegate : UIResponder <UIApplicationDelegate>
    ```

4. Select the CTAppDelegate.m file and change the comment on line 2 from AppDelegate.m to CTAppDelegate.m.

5. Change your import call from #import "AppDelegate.h" to #import "CTAppDelegate.h".

6. Change the class name of the implementation to CTAppDelegate.

    ```
    #import "CTAppDelegate.h"

    #import "MainViewController.h"

    @implementation CTAppDelegate
    ```

7. Select the iCloudTestApp-Prefix.pch file. This can be found under the Supporting Files group.

8. Just above the last #endif statement add a line and type:

    ```
    #import "CTAppDelegate.h"
    ```

9. Add two more lines above the #endif statement and type the following:

    ```
    #define AppDelegate (CTAppDelegate *)[[UIApplication sharedApplication] delegate]
    ```

The `#ifdef __OBJC__` should look like this:

```
#ifdef __OBJC__
    #import <UIKit/UIKit.h>
    #import <Foundation/Foundation.h>
    #import <CoreData/CoreData.h>
    #import "CTAppDelegate.h"

    #define AppDelegate (CTAppDelegate *)[[UIApplication sharedApplication] delegate]
#endif
```

10. Now select the `main.m` file inside the Support Files group.

11. Change the `import` statement from `AppDelegate` to `CTAppDelegate`.

12. Change the `[AppDelegate class]` to `[CTAppDelegate class]`.

```
#import <UIKit/UIKit.h>

#import "CTAppDelegate.h"

int main(int argc, char * argv[])
{
    @autoreleasepool {
        return UIApplicationMain(argc, argv, nil, NSStringFromClass([CTAppDelegate
class]));
    }
}
```

Now let's walk through this process. The first thing we did was rename our `AppDelegate` files to `CTAppDelegate`. We did this because we want the filename to be the same as the class name. Next we changed the class name from `AppDelegate` to `CTAppDelegate`. This is done because we want to access our Application Delegate with the name `AppDelegate` so it is easily understood what the variable is.

Then we added the define directive inside the precompiled headers file. This directive creates a macro that tells the compiler to replace the code we defined in all places that we call the defined identifier. In our case we will use `AppDelegate` to access our Application Delegate instead of writing `(CTAppDelegate *)[[UIApplication sharedApplication] delegate]`. We provided the import for the `CTAppDelegate` as well so that the compiler understands what `CTAppDelegate` is.

The final step was to update `main.m` with the correct entry point for the app. Setting the `UIApplicationMain` methods fourth parameter to `NSStringFromClass([CTAppDelegate class])` tells main that `CTAppDelegate` is the name of the class that our delegate is instantiated from. Basically, this is where our app starts.

Setting Up Your Storyboard

Now let's make a few modifications to our storyboard so that we have the objects already created that we will reference in code. Set up your storyboard file and save as shown in Figure 4-14.

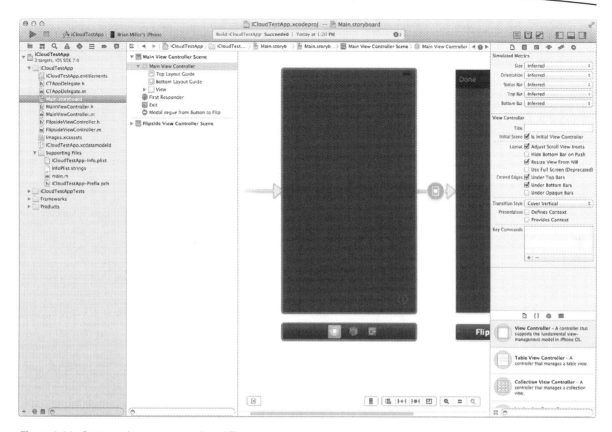

Figure 4-14. Create and save your storyboard files

1. Select the Main.storyboard to open the Visual editor.

2. Set up the MainViewController (Figure 4-15). Select the
    MainViewController from the Document Outline. If you don't see the
    Document Outline, select Editor ➤ Show Document Outline from the Xcode
    menu or click the button in the bottom left of the editor that looks like caret
    symbol facing right surrounded by a rectangle.

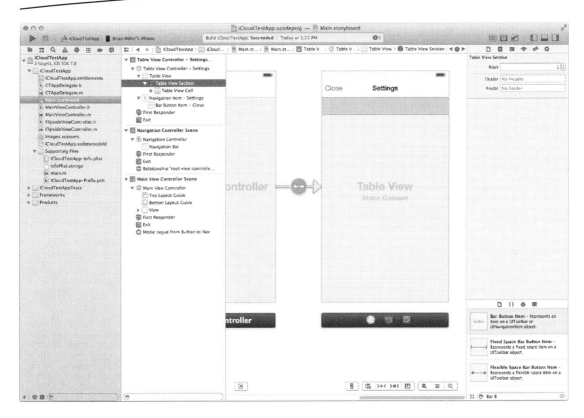

Figure 4-15. Main view controller

3.   Select the view (Figure 4-16).

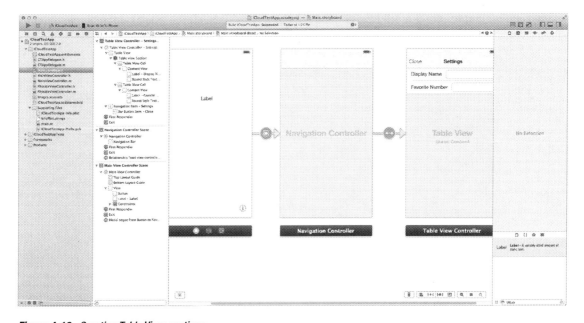

Figure 4-16. Creating Table View sections

4. With the view selected, change the background color to white from the Attributes Inspector on the right side of the screen.

5. Drag a label from the Object Library onto the `MainViewController`.

6. In the Attribute Inspector, change the alignment to centered.

7. Change Lines to **0**. Setting lines to 0 tells the label that it will have unlimited lines.

8. Change the dimensions of the label to **x:20 y:114 width:280 height:105**. You can set these by selecting the Size Inspector tab in the Utilities Pane.

Now it's time to set up the Segue:

1. Select the segue that is between the `MainViewController` and the `FlipSideViewController`.

2. In the Attributes Inspector, change the Identifier to ToSettings.

Next we set up the `FlipSideViewController`:

1. Select the `FlipSideViewController`.

2. From the menu, select Editor ➤ Embed In ➤ Navigation Controller.

3. Delete the `FlipSideViewController` because we really want a Table View Controller.

Finally, we set up the `SettingsViewController`:

1. Drag a Table View Controller from the Object Library on to the storyboard.

2. Ctrl-drag from the Navigation Control to the new Table View Controller you just added. When you release, you will be shown a menu. Left-click root view controller under Relationship Segue.

3. Select the Navigation Item inside the Table View Controller Scene in the Document Outline.

4. In the Attributes Inspector type **Settings** for title.

5. Drag a Bar Button Item to the left side of the Navigation Bar.

6. In the Attributes Inspector change the title to **Close**.

7. Select the Table View from the Document Outline.

8. Change the content in the Attributes Inspector to Static Cells.

9. Select the Table View Section inside the Table View in the Document Outline. You may need to expand the Table View contents by clicking the caret that is just to the left of it.

10. Change Rows to 1 in the Attribute Inspector.

11. Drag a Label into the Table View Cell.

12. Change the dimensions of the label to **x:15 y:11 width:112 height:21**.

13. Change the text Label to **Display Name**.

14. Now drag a Text Field into the Table View Cell.

15. Change the dimensions of the text field to **x:135 y:7 width:170 height:30**.

16. Select the Table View Section inside the Table View.

17. Change Rows to 2.

Note   We changed the rows to 1, made our cell, and then changed rows to 2 because it will copy the previous cell and paste it as any new cell, which saves us a little work.

18. Select the label inside the second cell and change it to **Favorite Number**. See Figure 4-17.

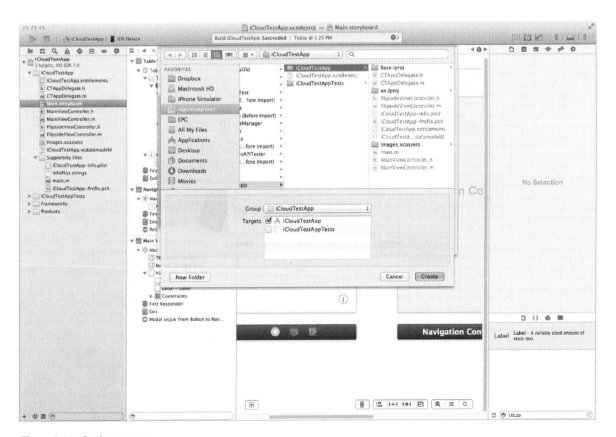

Figure 4-17. Settings screen

19.   Change the width of the cell to **132**.

20.   Select the text field and change the width to **150** and the x to **155**.

It Is Time for Some Code!

We can now write some code. We start off by removing the `FlipSideViewController` files because we no longer need them. Next, we create a constants file that store constants that we use when dealing with user defaults. Then we make some edits to the `CTAppDelegate` files so that we can set up our user defaults and save them. Moving on, we will edit the `MainViewController` file to handle the label that displays our welcome text. And finally we create a new `UITableViewController` to call `SettingsViewController`. It handles the text input on the Settings screen and also handles calling the methods that we created in the Application Delegate to handle saving our user defaults.

Constants File

The use of a constants file is common in object-oriented programming. This process allows us to set up either class-based static values or global static values for use in our code. In this case, we go the global route because our project is a simple app.

1.   Select File ➤ New ➤ File. . . from the Xcode menu.

2.   Under iOS, select Cocoa Touch.

3.   From the screen on the right select Objective-C Class and click Next.

4.   Name this class Constants.

5.   Set Subclass of to **NSObject** if not already set and click Next.

6.   In the Finder window, be sure that the class is going to be saved inside your project.

7.   Under Targets, be sure that iCloudTestApp is checked and click Create.

We can go ahead and delete the interface and the implementation in the corresponding `Constants.h` and `Constants.m` files because we won't need those.

Now define two constants: `CTDisplayName` and `CTFavoriteNumber`. In `Constants.h` add the following two lines:

```
NSString * const CTDisplayNameKey;
NSString * const CTFavoriteNumberKey;
```

In the `Constants.m` file give these variables values by adding the following:

```
NSString * const CTDisplayNameKey = @"DISPLAY_NAME";
NSString * const CTFavoriteNumberKey = @"FAVORITE_NUMBER";
```

The last thing we do is add an import command in the iCloudTestApp-Prefix.pch file. We will add it just after our import for CTAppDelegate.h. Your ifdef __OBJC__ block should now look like this:

```
#ifdef __OBJC__
    #import <UIKit/UIKit.h>
    #import <Foundation/Foundation.h>
    #import <CoreData/CoreData.h>
    #import "CTAppDelegate.h"
    #import "Constants.h"

    #define AppDelegate (CTAppDelegate *)[[UIApplication sharedApplication] delegate]
#endif
```

> **Note**   Why should we use constants? Using constants lets us change the value down the road without
> having to change any of the code that accesses the constant. The other important aspect of this is that we
> ensure that the constant cannot be changed by the running program at any time. It will actually throw a
> compiler error if you try to change the constant value.

Application Delegate and NSUserDefaults

NSUserDefaults is a local key-value store provided by iOS. Its intended use is to store settings that help determine the application's default state. In our case we will use it to store the user's display name and his favorite number.

Because we want to be sure these defaults exist when the application starts, it makes the most sense to start in the application delegate. We will start off by writing a method to check whether our user defaults exist:

```
- (BOOL)hasDefaults {
    BOOL hasDefaults = YES;

    if([[NSUserDefaults standardUserDefaults] stringForKey:CTDisplayName] == nil)
        hasDefaults = NO;
    else if([[NSUserDefaults standardUserDefaults] stringForKey:CTFavoriteNumber] == nil)
        hasDefaults = NO;

    return hasDefaults;
}
```

We start by creating a BOOL variable hasDefaults and setting it to YES. We then check to see whether each default value exists. If it does not, then we set our hasDefaults value to NO. The method then returns the value of hasDefaults.

Here is the extracted version of getting a userDefault:

```
NSUserDefaults *userDefaults = [NSUserDefaults standardUserDefaults];
NSString *value = [userDefaults stringForKey:@"DISPLAY_NAME"];
```

As you can see we start out by getting the NSUserDefaults object by calling the class method standardUserDefaults on the NSUserDefaults class. This method returns the shared defaults object.

Then we call the instance method stringForKey: on the NSUserDefaults object. There are other instance methods that you can use to get other object types out of the user defaults store. In our hasDefaults method we combine these two lines into one call. Both produce the same output.

Next we need to create a method that will set these user defaults if they do not exist. This method is important because we want to know that our defaults exist, even if the application is running for the first time.

```
- (void)createDefaults {
    NSUserDefaults *userDefaults = [NSUserDefaults standardUserDefaults];
    NSDictionary *appDefaults = @{CTDisplayName:@"John Doe",CTFavoriteNumber:@1};
    [userDefaults registerDefaults:appDefaults];
}
```

We start off by getting our NSUserDefaults object as we discussed previously. We then create a dictionary to hold our key value pairs. Finally, we create those by calling the instance method registerDefaults: on the NSUserDefaults object and passing our appDefaults dictionary as the parameter.

Our final step is to add our login inside the application:didFinishLaunchingWithOptions method of our application delegate. The first thing we want to do when this method is called is determine whether our defaults exist. If they don't, then we need to create them. Add these lines at the top of this method:

```
if(![self hasDefaults])
    [self createDefaults];
```

The first thing we want to do when we launch the app is to determine if our defaults exist by calling the hasDefaults method. If they don't then we create them by calling the createDefaults method. We are now done setting up our user defaults. It is necessary to do this because there has to be a default set. Our application is going to check whether there is one set, so we always know there has been one set.

Main View Controller

Now that we have our constants and our user defaults set up we want to be able to show the user what those defaults are set to. We display a welcome message using the user's default values.

Let's start by cleaning up some of the default code that was added for us.

In the MainViewController.h file remove the import command for the FlipsideViewController.h. Also remove the delegate FlipsideViewControllerDelegate adoption. MainViewController.h should now look like this:

```
#import <CoreData/CoreData.h>

@interface MainViewController : UIViewController

@property (strong, nonatomic) NSManagedObjectContext *managedObjectContext;

@end
```

In the MainViewController.m file remove the lines starting at #pragma mark — Flipside View all the way down to right after the prepareForSegue:sender: method.

Now that we are done getting rid of the things we don't need, it is time to add the things that we do need. Let's start by defining a property for the UILabel that we added to the view in the storyboard.

Inside the MainViewController private interface in the MainViewController.m file let's add the following property:

```
@property (weak, nonatomic) IBOutlet UILabel *lblWelcome;
```

We define this object as weak because the storyboard handles the instantiation for us so we don't need to create a strong reference to it. We will connect this outlet a little later.

Now we want to add a new method to handle updating the label with the properly formatted welcome message. We call this method updateUI:

```
-(void)updateUI {
    NSUserDefaults *userDefaults = [NSUserDefaults standardUserDefaults];
    _lblWelcome.text = [NSString stringWithFormat:@"Welcome %@\nYour favorite number is
%@",[userDefaults stringForKey:CTDisplayName],[userDefaults stringForKey:CTFavoriteNumber]];
}
```

As we have done previously, we start by getting a reference to the NSUserDefaults object. Then we assign formatted text to our UILabel using our constants to access the proper NSUserDefault value.

Next we extend the viewWillAppear:animated method and call our updateUI method inside of it:

```
-(void)viewWillAppear:(BOOL)animated {
    [super viewWillAppear:animated];

    [self updateUI];
}
```

The reason that we update the UI in the viewWillAppear: method, instead of the viewDidLoad: method is because we know that we are going to be editing the user defaults inside the SettingsViewController, previously known as the FlipsideViewController. This way every time the view is displayed it updates the label and we see our changes take effect immediately.

Goodbye FlipsideViewController, Hello SettingsViewController

This is our final step in laying the base foundation for our app. We start of by deleting the FlipsideViewController and creating a new class called SettingsViewController, which subclasses UITableViewController. In this view controller we create some UITextField properties. We also implement the UITextFieldDelegate protocol so we can interact with the text fields when certain events happen. We also create a method that is called from the Bar Button Item when it is pressed.

Let's start by deleting the FlipsideViewController.h and FlipsideViewController.m files. When prompted you can select Move to trash because we won't be needing these files anymore.

Now we need to create our `SettingsViewController` class.

1. Click File ➤ New ➤ File from the Xcode menu.

2. Select create a new Objective-C Class and click Next. For Subclass of select `UITableViewController`.

3. Type `SettingsViewController` for the Class and click Next.

4. In the Finder window be sure that the file is being saved in your project folder and be sure that `iCloudTestApp` is checked as the Target.

This class comes with a lot of boilerplate code that we don't need. Delete everything from the line #pragma mark—Table view data source all the way down to just before @end. The reason we don't need these methods is because we told the Storyboard that we were going to use Static cells—therefore we don't need any of the data source or delegate methods.

In the `SettingsViewController.m` file we want to create two properties for the text fields that we added. Add these two properties inside the private interface:

```
@property (weak, nonatomic) IBOutlet UITextField *txtDisplayName;
@property (weak, nonatomic) IBOutlet UITextField *txtFavoriteNumber;
```

We want these fields to already be filled in with the value we added to user defaults. We will create a method called `updateUI` that will handle setting the text fields:

```
-(void)updateUI {
    _txtDisplayName.text = [[NSUserDefaults standardUserDefaults] stringForKey:CTDisplayName];
    _txtFavoriteNumber.text = [[NSUserDefaults standardUserDefaults] stringForKey:CTFavoriteNumber];
}
```

You should be getting used to getting these values from `NSUserDefaults` by now.

We will follow the exact same process as we did in the `MainViewController` for calling this `updateUI` method. Add the `viewWillAppear:animated` method and call our `updateUI` method within it:

```
-(void)viewWillAppear:(BOOL)animated {
    [super viewWillAppear:animated];

    [self updateUI];
}
```

Now that we have displaying our values out of the way, we need to implement some methods that handle the inputting and changing of the values in the text fields. First we will write a method that will save the text field value to our user defaults. We will branch from this method later and show its importance. It would be less code to set these values, but because what we will implement with KVS, we want minimize the saves to the KVS store.

```
-(void)updateDefaultForTextField:(UITextField *)textField {
    NSUserDefaults *userDefaults = [NSUserDefaults standardUserDefaults];
    if([textField isEqual:_txtDisplayName]){
        if(![[userDefaults stringForKey:CTDisplayName] isEqualToString:textField.text]){
            [userDefaults setObject:textField.text forKey:CTDisplayName];
            [userDefaults synchronize];
        }
    } else {
        if(![[userDefaults stringForKey:CTFavoriteNumber] isEqualToString:textField.text]){
            [userDefaults setObject:[NSNumber numberWithFloat:[textField.text floatValue]]
forKey:CTFavoriteNumber];
            [userDefaults synchronize];
        }
    }
}
```

We start off by grabbing the reference to our NSUserDefaults object. We then add an if statement to check whether we are working with _txtDisplayName textfield or _txtFavoriteNumber. We use this to determine which key we should be working with. Then we check the current text field value against the userDefaults value to determine whether a change has in fact been made. If a change was made, we set the new value in userDefaults and call synchronize. The synchronize method is what forces the save to take place in NSUserDefaults; otherwise the OS invokes this method automatically at periodic intervals.

Next we adopt the UITextFieldDelegate protocol. Adopting this protocol tells the compiler that we intend to act as the delegate for a UITextField and that we will implement all required delegate methods as well as any optional methods. If your class does not completely conform to the protocol, the compiler will give you warnings letting you know. Select the SettingsViewController.h file and change the interface definition to this:

```
@interface SettingsViewController : UITableViewController <UITextFieldDelegate>
```

In the SettingsViewController.m file we need to add one optional UITextFieldDelegate method. The method we implement is textFieldShouldReturn:. This method is called when the user presses Return on the keyboard. We use this method to change the first responder. In our case the first responder is the object that will be responding to the keyboard. We will also add a pragma mark above this method so that we can easily find it in the jump bar.

```
#pragma mark - UITextFieldDelegate Methods
- (BOOL)textFieldShouldReturn:(UITextField *)textField {
    [self updateDefaultForTextField:textField];

    if([textField isEqual:_txtDisplayName])
        [_txtFavoriteNumber becomeFirstResponder];
    else
        [_txtFavoriteNumber resignFirstResponder];

    return YES;
}
```

The first parameter of this method gives us the UITextField that called it. We start off by calling our updateDefaultForTextField method and passing it the textField object. We then use the isEqual method on NSObject: to determine if we are working with the _txtDisplayName object. If we are, then we call the method becomeFirstResponder on our _txtFavoriteNumber object. This causes the focus to change to our _txtFavoriteNumber object and displays the keyboard if it is not already being displayed. The else portion of the statement is used if this method was called by _txtFavoriteNumber. If that is the case, then we call the resignFirstResponder. This causes the focus to move from the text field and causes the keyboard to hide.

We are almost done, but we haven't handled the Bar Button Item that we will use to leave the view. To handle the Close button press, we will add two methods. The first method simply calls our updateDefaultTextField: method on each of our text fields to handle our saving of the data. We call this method updateAllTextFields.

```
-(void)updateAllDefaults {
    [self updateDefaultForTextField:_txtDisplayName];
    [self updateDefaultForTextField:_txtFavoriteNumber];
}
```

Now we add a method called btnClose: that calls our updateAllDefaults method and also dismisses our view controller, which returns us to our MainViewController. We add another pragma mark above it for good organization.

```
#pragma mark - Button Methods
-(IBAction)btnClosePressed:(id)sender {
    [self updateAllDefaults];

    [self dismissViewControllerAnimated:YES completion:nil];
}
```

The only thing new here is that we are calling an instance method dismissViewControllerAnimated :completion: against our SettingsViewController. This method has two parameters: a BOOL and a code block. We want to set the first parameter to YES so that we get the nice reverse animation that is used when we move to this view. Set the second parameter to nil because we don't want to do anything once the view has been dismissed.

Back to the Storyboard

The last thing we need to do is make some connections in our storyboard and we will be ready to test the app. Go ahead and select Main.storyboard in the Project Navigator.

1. Select MainViewController in the Document Outline.

2. Expand the View so you can see the Label and the Button.

3. Ctrl-drag from the Main View Controller to the Label and select lblWelcome.

4. Select the SettingsViewController in the Document Outline.

5. Show the Identity Inspector in the Utilities pane.

6. Change Class to `SettingsViewController`.

7. Ctrl-drag from the Settings View Controller to the first text field and select `txtDisplayName`.

8. Ctrl-drag from the first text field to the Settings View Controller and select `delegate` under Outlets.

9. Ctrl-drag from the Settings View Controller to the second text field and select `txtFavoriteNumber`.

10. Ctrl-drag from the second text field to the Settings View Controller and select delegate under Outlets.

11. Ctrl-drag from the Close Bar Button Item to Settings View Controller and select "`btnClosePressed:`" under Sent Actions.

Now you can build and run your app in the simulator. You should see the defaults when you first open the app. Pressing the "I" button will take you to the Settings screen where you can change the values for Display Name and Favorite Number. When you press the Close button in the navigation bar you will be taken back to the Main Screen. You should immediately see the new Display Name and Favorite Number that you entered in the Settings screen as shown in Figures 4-18 through 4-20.

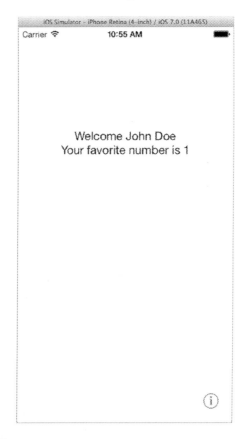

Figure 4-18. Initial screen of your app

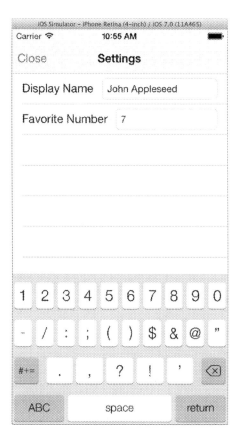

Figure 4-19. Settings screen of your app

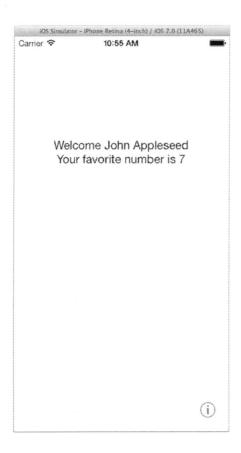

Figure 4-20. Your favorite number

Key-Value Store

Now it's time to dive into iCloud using the Key-Value Store. iCloud gives us two models to work with: the Key-Value Store and the Document Store. Let's start off with the Key-Value Store because it is by far the most basic to implement. The iCloud Key-Value Store is very similar to the NSUserDefaults we are already using. It is an NSDictionary in the cloud, or more precisely, iCloud.

The iCloud Key-Value Store is recommended to only be used for app preferences, app configuration, or app state. The Key-Value store is available to every instance of your app on all the user's devices. So, when a user updates a value on one instance of the app, the other instances will be notified of this change and can update accordingly.

Each time you write a value to this store, the operation will either succeed or fail automatically. This means that if you need to ensure that all the values you want to save are actually saved, you can package them in a dictionary. If any of the values inside the dictionary fail to save, none of the values will be saved.

iCloud automatically handles conflicts by delivering you the most up-to-date value for any keys based on timestamp. For this reason, it is recommended that you use NSUserDefaults in concert with iCloud Key-Value Store. This allows you to resolve any conflicts that could arise from situations where one device may update a value before it receives the previously updated value.

To understand this, here is a simple example: Device A has been running your app for 15 days and updates the key DAYS_RAN to 15. Now device B starts running the app and it updates DAYS_RAN to 1. If you rely solely on iCloud, and device A receives the updated value, your DAYS_RAN will be set to 1. By using NSUserDefaults you can check that updated value and determine that 15 is more accurate than 1 and resolve the conflict yourself by setting the iCloud value back to 15.

There are some restrictions to this Key-Value Store that you should be aware of. The overall data you are able to store is limited to 1MB per user. You are also limited to 1024 key-value pairs per user. This means that you could have one single key-value pair that is 1MB or you could have 1,000 key-value pairs that are 1KB each. If you exceed this quota, your app will be notified and you can handle it appropriately. This data does not count against the user's iCloud storage, rather, this storage is independent to your app.

Key-Value Stores can be used to store scalar values such as BOOL and int as well as property-list types: NSNumber, NSString, NSDate, NSData, NSArray, and NSDictionary. It is important to note that the maximum length of a key string is 64 bytes using UTF8 encoding.

NSUbiquitousKeyValueStore

You can access this Key-Value Store in code by referencing the NSUbiquitousKeyValueStore class object. To get the store we call the class method defaultStore. Let's start off by adding a public method in CTAppDelegate to save a key-value pair to the store. In CTAppDelegate.h add the following instance method declaration just after the declaration for applicationDocumentsDirectory.

```
- (void)updateKeyValueStoreKey:(NSString *)key withObject:(id)object;
```

Now in CTAppDelegate.m we need to add the implementation to this method.

```
- (void)updateKeyValueStoreKey:(NSString *)key withObject:(id)object {
    NSUbiquitousKeyValueStore *kvStore = [NSUbiquitousKeyValueStore defaultStore];
    [kvStore setObject:object forKey:key];
}
```

This is a pretty basic method but let's walk through it anyway. Our method takes in a string key and an object. We start off by grabbing a reference to our app's NSUbiquitousKeyValueStore object by calling [NSUbiquitousKeyValueStore defaultStore]. We then call the instance method setObject:forKey on our default store passing in the key and object that our method has received.

Setting objects does not automatically write those values back out to iCloud. It only writes them to the local ubiquitous container. Changes in this ubiquitous container are written to iCloud at a schedule determined by the operating system. You can however explicitly force this synchronization by calling the instance method synchronize on your NSUbiquitousKeyValueStore object. Let's add a public method to force that synchronization now by adding the method definition in our CTAppDelegate.h file:

```
- (void)syncKVStore;
```

Now let's add our method implementation in CTAppDelegate.m:

```
- (void)syncKVStore {
    [[NSUbiquitousKeyValueStore defaultStore] synchronize];
}
```

It is important to note that when your app starts you should call synchronize immediately so that your app knows to check the iCloud Key-Value Store for changes at launch. Let's add this method call in the application:didFinishLaunchingWithOptions: method right after we verify that our defaults are created:

```
- (BOOL)application:(UIApplication *)application didFinishLaunchingWithOptions:(NSDictionary *)
launchOptions
{
    if(![self hasDefaults])
        [self createDefaults];


    [self syncKVStore];

    //Comment: Override point for customization after application launch.

    MainViewController *controller = (MainViewController *)self.window.rootViewController;
    controller.managedObjectContext = self.managedObjectContext;
    return YES;
}
```

Now that we can write to it, how do we know if there are any changes? To be notified of changes we need to add an observer to NSNotificationCenter. We want to listen for the message NSUbiquitousKeyValueStoreDidChangeExternallyNotification. Let's add the following code just after our user defaults check, but before the syncKVStore method call in the application:didFinish LaunchingWithOptions: method:

```
//Comment: Register for Key-Value Store Notifications
    [[NSNotificationCenter defaultCenter] addObserver:self selector:@selector(storeDidChange:)
name:NSUbiquitousKeyValueStoreDidChangeExternallyNotification object:[NSUbiquitousKeyValueStore
defaultStore]];
```

Here we call the method addObserver:selector:name:object on our NSNotificationCenter object to tell our default notification center that we want to listen for these messages and respond to them. The first parameter we provide is our Application Delegate object that defines that we will be the one listening for this message. The second parameter we provide is the method selector that we want to call when this message is received. We have not added that method yet, but we will shortly. The third parameter provided is the name of the message we are listening for. And the final parameter is the object sender that we provide our iCloud Key-Value Store object.

Now we need to add the method storeDidChange:, which will really be the meat of our logic. This is where you can test for conflicts and do any other logic to keep your user defaults and the iCloud Key-Value Store in sync. Let's add that method now.

```
- (void)storeDidChange:(NSNotification *)notification {
    // Get the list of keys that did change
    NSDictionary *userInfo = [notification userInfo];
    NSNumber *reasongForChange = [userInfo objectForKey:NSUbiquitousKeyValueStoreChangeReasonKey];
    NSInteger reason = -1;
```

If a reason could not be determined, we shouldn't update anything.

```
if(!reasongForChange)
    return;
```

Now you will update only for changes from the server.

```
    reason = [reasongForChange integerValue];
    if(reason == NSUbiquitousKeyValueStoreServerChange || reason ==
NSUbiquitousKeyValueStoreInitialSyncChange){
        NSArray *changedKeys = [userInfo objectForKey:NSUbiquitousKeyValueStoreChangedKeysKey];
        NSUbiquitousKeyValueStore *kvStore = [NSUbiquitousKeyValueStore defaultStore];
        NSUserDefaults *userDefaults = [NSUserDefaults standardUserDefaults];

        [changedKeys enumerateObjectsUsingBlock:^(NSString *key, NSUInteger idx, BOOL *stop) {
            id value = [kvStore objectForKey:key];
            [userDefaults setObject:value forKey:key];
        }];
    }
}
```

This is a lot at first glance, but it will quickly make sense. This method receives an NSNotification object. This is the object that is sent to us whenever the message NSUbiquitousKeyValueStoreDidChangeExternallyNotification is received by the app. We start off by calling the userInfo method to get the data or payload of the notification. It comes in the form of an NSDictionary. We then extract the reason for change by getting the value for the key NSUbiquitousKeyValueStoreChangeReasonKey. The reason is in the form of an NSNumber which we assign to the variable reasonForChange. Then we set up an NSInteger variable "reason" and assign it a value of -1. Setting this to -1 ensures that it doesn't conflict with any of the enum values that we will check for. We then do a check to make sure that our reasonForChange is not nil. If it is, we return out of this method. If not, we continue on and pull out the integerValue and assign it to reason.

Note Apple provides two constants to us for working with the userInfo dictionary of the NSUbiquitousKeyValueStoreDidChangeExternallyNotification notification. They are NSUbiquitousKeyValueStoreChangeReasonKey and NSUbiquitousKeyValueStoreChangedKeysKey.

In the if block we are checking for two change reasons NSUbiquitousKeyValueStoreServerChange and NSUbiquitousKeyValueStoreInitialSyncChange. The ServerChange reason is what we will receive when another instance of the app has updated, added, or removed a key-value pair. InitialSyncChange is delivered if this is our first sync on this device. In both of these instances we want to retrieve those values and write them to our NSUserDefaults.

Once we know we have a change we care about, we need to get the keys for those changes. We get these by getting the object for the key NSUbiquitousKeyValueStoreChangedKeysKey and assigning it to an NSArray we call changedKeys. Then we create a reference to our iCloud Key-Value Store and our User Defaults Store so we can work with them.

We can now enumerate through each of the keys in the changedKeys array and write those key-value pairs to our user defaults. We call objectForKey: on kvStore and pass it the current key assigning the object to the variable value. Next, we call the method setObject:forKey: on userDefaults to assign the value to the proper key.

That is all there is to it. We are now set up to receive changes from the iCloud Key-Value Store and write changes to them. You may notice though, that we haven't called our method updateKeyValue StoreKey:withObject yet. Let's move over to the SettingsViewController.m file and make quick modifications.

We should start by adding another private property called isChanged that is a BOOL value.

@property BOOL isChanged; Now want to update our instance method updateDefaultForTextField: to call the updateKeyValueStoreKey:withObject method in our Application Delegate. We do this by first checking to see whether synchronizing our user defaults was successful. If it was, then we will update the key-value store and set our new isChanged BOOL value to YES. Our method should now look like this:

```
-(void)updateDefaultForTextField:(UITextField *)textField {
    NSUserDefaults *userDefaults = [NSUserDefaults standardUserDefaults];
    if([textField isEqual:_txtDisplayName]){
        if(![[userDefaults stringForKey:CTDisplayName] isEqualToString:textField.text]){
            [userDefaults setObject:textField.text forKey:CTDisplayName];
            if([userDefaults synchronize])
                [AppDelegate updateKeyValueStoreKey:CTDisplayName withObject:textField.text];

            _isChanged = YES;
        }
    } else {
        if(![[userDefaults stringForKey:CTFavoriteNumber] isEqualToString:textField.text]){
            [userDefaults setObject:[NSNumber numberWithFloat:[textField.text floatValue]]
forKey:CTFavoriteNumber];
            if([userDefaults synchronize])
                [AppDelegate updateKeyValueStoreKey:CTFavoriteNumber withObject:textField.text];

            _isChanged = YES;
        }
    }
}
```

As you can see we are now using our `AppDelegate` #define that we added in our iCloudTestApp-Prefix.pch file. This makes the call to `updateKeyValueStoreKey:withObject` a lot easier to read.

The last thing we need to do is update our `btnClosePressed:` method. We want to call the `syncKVStore` method on our Application Delegate after the dismissal is complete. But, we only want to call this if a change actually took place because we don't want to be flooding the store with sync calls when nothing has changed. The method should now look like this:

```
#pragma mark - Button Methods
-(IBAction)btnClosePressed:(id)sender {
    [self updateAllDefaults];

    [self dismissViewControllerAnimated:YES completion:^{
        if(_isChanged)
            [AppDelegate syncKVStore];
    }];
}
```

This completes the iCloud Key-Value Store implementation, but we still have one small problem. Because the Key-Value Store updates can happen at any time while the app is running, we should also configure our UI to handle that. This is an easy task to handle with NSNotificationCenter. Similar to the way we added ourselves as listeners for the `NSUbiquitousKeyValueStoreDidChangeExternallyNotification` message we can add ourselves as listeners to a message that we will actually create.

We will start by adding another constant declaration in our `Constants.h` file:

```
extern NSString * const UIShouldRefresh;
```

Also, don't forget to add the implementation in the `Constants.m` file:

```
NSString * const UIShouldRefresh = @"UI_SHOULD_REFRESH";
```

Now let's go back to the `CTAppDelegate.m` file and modify our `storeDidChange:` method by adding the following invocation inside the `if` statement we use to check if there is a change we care about.

```
[[NSNotificationCenter defaultCenter] postNotificationName:UIShouldRefresh object:nil];
```

Our final step is to set up our Main View Controller and Settings View Controller to listen for this message and respond. Inside each of these view controllers we will add the following line to the `viewWillAppear:` method.

```
[[NSNotificationCenter defaultCenter] addObserver:self selector:@selector(updateUI:)
name:UIShouldRefresh object:nil];
```

When you set a class as an observer for a notification it is best practice to remove yourself as an observer when you don't need to be. It is important to remember that even though the view controller isn't on-screen, it doesn't mean that it has been removed from memory and isn't accessible. In our case we only care about listening for the message `UIShouldRefresh` when the view controller is actually being displayed. Because of that, let's implement the `viewDidDisappear:` method and remove ourselves as an observer.

```
-(void)viewDidDisappear:(BOOL)animated {
    [super viewDidDisappear:animated];

    //Comment: removes self from responding to any notifications

    [[NSNotificationCenter defaultCenter] removeObserver:self];
}
```

Now it is time to test our app again. You can test across multiple devices or you can test in the simulator by making some changes and then removing the app and re-installing it. It is important to remember that the iCloud Key-Value Store is not immediate. iOS determines when updates are retrieved and even when calling synchronize, it can take anywhere from a few seconds to up to an hour to receive notification of a change.

Summary

From this chapter, you have gained a fundamental understanding of the intricacies in adding iCloud support to an app. You've learned the importance of App IDs, provisioning profiles, and entitlements. You should now be able to start an app project from scratch and set it up to work with iCloud.

The Key-Value Store is an important start in learning and becoming versed in all that iCloud has to offer you. Apple has provided you with a simple, but effective API to update your app's Key-Value Store and respond to changes made by other instances of your app.

In the following chapters I will explain how to integrate CoreData as well as UIDocuments into your apps. I also discuss different methods you can use to test these technologies and ensure that you are getting the results you are expecting.

iCloud Document Storage with UIDocument

In this chapter you will learn the fundamentals of adding iCloud Document Storage to your applications. I start by explaining what the iCloud Document storage is and how it has been integrated into core technologies for you to leverage. In discussing these technologies I show you the two different ways that you can take your application to iCloud by using UIDocument and Core Data.

Next we dive into detail on both of these technologies. Using our test app from the previous chapter we will add a new section that uses UIDocument at the local level. I then modify the app to show you how you can move those local documents to iCloud.

Because Core Data is such a complex technology I highly recommend using other materials completely devoted to it. We will add a third section to our application that utilizes a Core Data backend. And just like we did for UIDocument, we take Core Data and move it to the iCloud.

iCloud Document Storage

iCloud Document Storage utilizes a Document Service that exists on all devices. This service orchestrates the persistence of data from a special directory on the device and the iCloud server. The service sends your application messages, alerting you to changes through the iCloud Storage API.

I know it may sound too simple to be true, but it actually is that simple. The engineers at Apple have taken care of all of the server side code for you. You don't have to worry about load balancing, replication, disaster recovery, or anything else that you would normally need to think about when implementing a server technology. So, with that said let's go a little deeper.

Ubiquity Container

The Ubiquity Container is sometimes referred to as the iCloud container. It is a physically separate folder or container on the device to which your application has access. Any file data that your application puts into the container will be uploaded to iCloud and pushed down to the users' other devices that have your app installed.

The container is first created when you request the container URL from the iCloud Storage API. You should also never call this method on the main thread because it will lock the UI.

When you first put a file into the container, the entire document is uploaded to iCloud. If that document changes for any reason only certain pieces of that file are sent up to iCloud to trigger those changes. This method allows iCloud to remain efficient while keeping all the documents it handles up to date.

Document Metadata

One of the nice features of iCloud is how it handles your file metadata. Your files' metadata take precedence over the actual data contained inside the document. The document service is very aggressive about pushing metadata to the cloud ahead of the actual changed data. What this means to you as a developer is that your application is going to be aware of all the files available to it even if that file's data hasn't been completely pushed to iCloud or downloaded to your device.

Document Data

The data within your document exists in iCloud until you explicitly request that it be downloaded. Once the file is downloaded, iCloud propagates any changes to the document down to your device. The document service handles document data this way in order to conserve storage space on your mobile device. So, suppose you have 100MB of documents stored in iCloud and you realize that you want to edit one that is 5MB. The document service only pulls down that individual file, leaving the other 95MB on the server. Now, your application is still aware of these other files thanks to the metadata being persisted across devices. This efficiency is one of the many reasons that iCloud is a superior technology to use in your iOS apps.

Peer to Peer

Another optimization that has been made for iCloud is the use of peer to peer technology. When you change a document on one device, that change can be sent over peer to peer connection to other devices rather than taking the full round trip to the iCloud servers and back down to each device. Peer to peer will only function when your devices are on the same network.

Conflict Resolution

Document Storage used automatic conflict resolution. What this means is that if you edit the same file on two different devices at the same time, iCloud will see that these edits are in conflict. It will resolve the conflict automatically by selecting what it believes is the most up to date file. However, you are also notified of this conflict. The iCloud Storage API gives you the ability to traverse through file versions and resolve the conflict manually if needed.

URL Publishing

iCloud also lets you request a public URL of your document. By using this URL you can allow others to view the file by sending the URL through other mediums such as e-mail and iMessage. It is important to note that the URL takes the user to a snapshot of the file at that moment in time. If the document is changed it will not be reflected by that previously generated URL. A new URL would need to be created to show that change. The URLs generated by the iCloud API are also only valid for a specific state and they are not permanent. The URL expires naturally over time.

Ubiquity Identity Token

The Ubiquity Identity Token is a token that is provided to you by the iCloud Storage API. The token references a particular user on a device within your app. This means that if you are signed into two different devices, the Ubiquity Token is different. Also, a token for a user in your app is not the same as the token of the same user in another app. You can use the Ubiquity Identity token to first confirm that the user has iCloud set up for their account. It can also be used to determine if a different user is now using your app on the same device.

Types of Documents

There are three types of documents supported with iCloud Document Storage. They are files, packages, and Core Data.

- Files can be any of the UNIX file types, as well as symlinks and directories.

- Packages on the other hand are multiple files in a single directory. A package consists of smaller individual files. Because of this granularity within the package, iCloud ends up sending fewer updates to the file as a whole.

- The third type is Core Data. Your Core Data store remains local, but your change logs are what is sent to iCloud.

Modifying Our Current Project for UIDocument Support

Now that I have explained what document storage is, we need to get our test application modified so that we can start adding the use of UIDocument inside it. We will be adding a UITabBarController as the root view of our app to divide our sections. Then we will add a UICollectionView to hold our documents.

Modifying the Storyboard

Let's get started.

1. Select the Main.storyboard to open the storyboard editor.

2. Select the MainViewController so that it is highlighted.

3. In the Xcode menu select Editor ➤ Embed In ➤ Tab Bar Controller. A new Tab Bar Controller is added to the storyboard that already has the first tab set as Main View Controller.

4.   Now drag a `UICollectionView` from the object library to your storyboard.

5.   With the new `UICollectionView` selected, embed a `UINavigationController` by selecting Editor ➤ Embed In ➤ Navigation Controller from the Xcode menu.

6.   Ctrl-drag from the Tab Bar Controller to the new `UINavigationController` and select View Controllers under Relationship Segue from the pop-up menu.

7.   Select the Tab Bar Item in the new `UINavigationController` and change the title to *Friends*.

8.   Now select the Tab Bar Item inside `MainViewController` and change the title to *Me*.

9.   Now drag a `UIViewController` from the object library and place it to the right of the Collection View Controller.

10. Ctrl-drag from the `UICollectionViewController` to the new `UIViewController` and select push from the pop-up menu.

Configuring the Collection View Controller

Now we need to configure the collection view controller:

1.   Select the Collection View inside the UICollectionView controller.

2.   In the Attribute Inspector, change the Background color of the view to White Color.

3.   Select the Size Inspector and change the Cell Size to width:140 and height:177.

4.   Change the section insets to top:8 bottom:8 left:8 right:8.

5.   Drag a Bar Button Item to the top right of the navigation bar and change its identifier to Add.

6.   Now drag a UIImageView from the object library into the `UICollectionViewCell`.

7.   Give the Image View a width and height of 140.

8.   Drag a UILabel from the object library into the `UICollectionViewCell`.

9.   Position it at x:0 y:148 width:140 height:21.

10. Select the Attribute Inspector and change the alignment to centered.

11. Set autoshrink to Minimum Font Scale and give it a value of 0.5.

12. Select the Navigation Item and set the title to *Friends*.

Configuring the Detail View Controller

Next configure the detail view controller:

1. Select the new `UIViewController`.

2. Drag a Bar Button Item from the object library to the right side of the `UINavigationBar` and set its title to *Edit*.

3. Now drag four text fields into the view.

4. Set them up as follows:

    a. First text field

        i. **Position & Size**: x:20 y:84 width:136 height:30

        ii. **Placeholder Text**: First Name

        iii. **Text Alignment**: Left

    b. Second text field

        i. **Position & Size**: x:164 y:84 width:136 height:30

        ii. **Placeholder Text**: Last Name

        iii. **Text Alignment**: Left

    c. Third text field

        i. **Position & Size**: x:20 y:122 width:181 height:30

        ii. **Placeholder Text**: Display Name

        iii. **Text Alignment**: Left

    d. Fourth text field

        i. **Position & Size**: x:209 y:122 width:91 height:30

        ii. **Placeholder Text**: Fav. Num.

        iii. **Text Alignment**: Right

5. Now drag a UIImageView from the object library and place it at x:20 y:160 width:280 height:280.

6. Under the Attribute Inspector check the User Interaction Enabled box.

7. Lastly, select the segue coming into the view and set its identifier to *ToFriendDetails*.

Adding Our Code Files

Now that we have our storyboard set up it is time to write the code that will control it. Let's start by creating a new Objective-C class that is a subclass of `UICollectionViewController`. Call it `FriendsCollectionViewController`.

We also need to create an Objective-C class for the Collection View Cell. Add another Objective-C class that is a subclass of `UICollectiionViewCell`. Let's call this one `EntryCollectionViewCell`.

Finally, we need to create another class for our `UIViewController` that will act as a detail view. Add another Objective-C class that is a subclass of `UIViewController` and name it `FriendDetailViewController`.

CTAppDelegate

In the `CTAppDelegate.m` file you need to delete two lines in the `application:didFinishLaunchingWith Options:` method. Here are the two lines you need to remove:

```
MainViewController *controller = (MainViewController *)self.window.rootViewController;
controller.managedObjectContext = self.managedObjectContext;
```

EntryCollectionViewCell

Let's open up the `EntryCollectionViewCell.h` file and start writing our interface. We first want to add a protocol definition just above the @interface line for our delegate protocol:

```
@protocol EntryCollectionViewCellDelegate;
```

Now add a method definition to configure the cell. Call this method `configureCellForEntry:withDel egate` and it takes an `NSString` and a `EntryCollectionViewCellDelegate` as its parameters:

```
-(void)configureCellForEntry:(NSString *)entry withDelegate:(id<EntryCollectionViewCellDelegate>)
delegate;
```

The final piece of code we want to add is our full protocol definition. We add a delegate method called `entryCollectionViewCell:longPressedForEntry` and it has an `EntryCollectionViewCell` and an `NSString` as its parameters.

```
@protocol EntryCollectionViewCellDelegate <NSObject>
-(void)entryCollectionViewCell:(EntryCollectionViewCell *)cell longPressedForEntry:(NSString *)
entry;
@end
```

You may be wondering why we define the protocol in two places rather than just using the preceding code by itself. Well, the reason is that we want to send back a reference to the cell and at the first protocol definition we don't know anything about `EntryCollectionViewCell` because the interface hasn't been defined yet. By adding the empty protocol we can reference the protocol inside the interface. Then when we add the protocol definition again we can reference the `EntryCollectionViewCell` object.

Let's now move over to the `EntryCollectionViewCell.m` file and make some more modifications. The first thing we want to do is create a private interface. We will add four properties inside it for our `UILabel`, `UIImageView`, `EntryCollectionViewDelegate`, and our `NSString`. We add `IBOutlet` commands to the label and image view so we can connect them in interface builder. The private interface should look like this:

```
@interface EntryCollectionViewCell()
@property (weak) IBOutlet UIImageView *imgPhoto;
@property (weak) IBOutlet UILabel *lblDisplayName;
@property (assign) id<EntryCollectionViewCellDelegate> delegate;
@property (assign) NSString *entry;
@end
```

Next we can remove all the boilerplate code inside the implementation. You should be left with only the @implementation line and the @end line.

We want to set up a `UILongPressGesture` Recognizer for this cell. Because our cell is instantiated from the storyboard, we will write the `initWithCoder` method and add our gesture recognizer addition there.

```
-(id)initWithCoder:(NSCoder *)aDecoder {
    if((self = [super initWithCoder:aDecoder])){
        UILongPressGestureRecognizer *longPress = [[UILongPressGestureRecognizer alloc]
initWithTarget:self action:@selector(longPressed:)];
        [self addGestureRecognizer:longPress];
    }

    return self;
}
```

In the `initWithCoder` method we created a long press gesture recognizer and added it to our self, the view. In the creation of the recognizer we reference an action method `longPressed:`. Let's write that method now.

```
-(void)longPressed:(UIGestureRecognizer *)gesture {
    if(gesture.state == UIGestureRecognizerStateBegan){
        [_delegate entryCollectionViewCell:self longPressedForEntry:_entry];
    }
}
```

As you can see, this is a very simple pass through method. But, there is one caveat that I want to point out. The first line of this method checks the state of the gesture. The reason we do this in this instance is that the recognizer will actually fire this method twice. It is called when the gesture begins and ends. Because we are only concerned with it when it begins, we check the state and only act on it when it is `UIGestureRecognizerStateBegan`. Once we know the state has begun, we call our delegate method on the registered delegate.

Now we need to add our `configureCellForEntry:withDelegate` implementation. In this method we will simply take the incoming variables and assign them to our local variables as long as entry is not nil. Then we will configure the image view and the label. Because we aren't handling an image right now, we will use the `ImgCellNoImage` for the time being.

```
-(void)configureCellForEntry:(NSString *)entry withDelegate:(id<EntryCollectionViewCellDelegate>)
delegate {
    if(entry == nil)
        return;

    _entry = entry;
    _delegate = delegate;

    _imgPhoto.image = [UIImage imageNamed:@"ImgCellNoImage"];
    _lblDisplayName.text = _entry;

}
```

The final class method that we want to override is `prepareForReuse`. This method is called right before a view is reused. Since we don't want any of the cell's previous data to display we use this method to reset the image view and the label. We also set our entry back to nil.

```
-(void)prepareForReuse {
    _entry = nil;
    _imgPhoto.image = nil;
    _lblDisplayName.text = @"";
}
```

Now is a good time to move back to the storyboard and connect everything for this cell. Follow these steps:

1. Select `Main.Storyboard`.

2. Select the `CollectionViewCell` inside the `UICollectionViewController`.

3. Under the Identity Inspector, change Class to `EntryCollectionViewCell`.

4. Under Attribute Inspector, set the Identifier to `EntryCollectionViewCell`.

5. Select the Connection Inspector.

6. Under outlets, click and drag from the little circle to the right of `imgPhoto` to the `UIImageView` in the cell.

7. Do the same thing for `lblDisplayName` and drag it to the label.

FriendsCollectionViewController

Open up the `FriendsCollectionViewController.h` file and add the `import` statement for `EntryCollectionViewCell.h`.

```
#import "EntryCollectionViewCell.h"
```

Next we want to tell the compiler that we will be conforming to three protocols:

- UICollectionViewDatasource
- UICollectionViewDelegate
- EntryCollectionViewCellDelegate

```
@interface FriendsCollectionViewController : UICollectionViewController <UICollectionViewDataSource,
UICollectionViewDelegate, EntryCollectionViewCellDelegate>
```

That's it for the interface. Now let's move on to the FriendsCollectionViewController.m file. We will start by adding a few properties to the private interface. These should be self-explanatory.

```
@interface FriendsCollectionViewController ()
@property (strong) NSMutableArray *entries;
@property (strong) NSString *selectedEntry;
@property BOOL shouldStartEditing;
@end
```

Also, go ahead and delete the initWithNibName:bundle method because we have no use for it. Inside the viewDidLoad method we need to initialize our entry's mutable array. Because this array will actually contain documents later, we can go ahead and just add some values in the initialization to get us what we need for now. Add the following line just after the [super viewDidLoad]; method call inside the viewDidLoad method:

```
_entries = @[@"Friend 1",@"Friend 2",@"Friend 3"].mutableCopy;
```

Now we need to add our UICollectionViewDatasource methods.

```
#pragma mark - UICollectionViewDatasource Methods
- (NSInteger)collectionView:(UICollectionView *)collectionView
numberOfItemsInSection:(NSInteger)section {
    return [_entries count];
}

- (NSInteger)numberOfSectionsInCollectionView:(UICollectionView *)collectionView {
    return 1;
}

- (UICollectionViewCell *)collectionView:(UICollectionView *)collectionView
cellForItemAtIndexPath:(NSIndexPath *)indexPath {

    EntryCollectionViewCell *cell = [collectionView
dequeueReusableCellWithReuseIdentifier:@"EntryCollectionViewCell" forIndexPath:indexPath];

    NSString *entry = _entries[indexPath.row];
    [cell configureCellForEntry:entry withDelegate:self];

    return cell;
}
```

We start out by adding a pragma mark so we can quickly find these methods from the jump bar. The first method we implement is `collectionView:numberOfItemsInSection`. Because we are only going to have one section, and our entries array will contain all the entries for that section, we just pass back the total number of entries we have by using the count method on our array.

Then we implement the `numberOfSectionsInCollectionView:` method. Again, we are only going to have one section so we send it back a value of 1.

The final method is `collectionView:cellForItemAtIndexPath:`. We start out by pulling out a `EntryCollectionViewCell` from the collection view by calling `dequeueReusableCellWithReuseId entifier:forIndexPath:`. This method returns either a new instantiated cell or a dequeued cell that has been prepared for reuse. Once we have the cell, we determine what entry we are concerned with by calling `_entries[indexPath.row]` to pull our entry out of the entries array. Then we call our helper method `configureCellForEntry:withDelegate:` and pass in the entry and ourselves as the delegate. Finally we return our configured cell.

The next thing we want to do is add our `UICollectionViewDelegate` Methods. We are actually only concerned with one method here which is the `collectionView:didSelectItemAtIndexPath:`.

```
#pragma mark - UICollectionViewDelegateFlowLayout Methods
- (void)collectionView:(UICollectionView *)collectionView didSelectItemAtIndexPath:(NSIndexPath *)
indexPath {
    NSString *entry = _entries[indexPath.row];

    _selectedEntry = entry;
    _shouldStartEditing = NO;

    [self performSegueWithIdentifier:@"ToFriendDetails" sender:nil];
}
```

We first get the selected entry by using the `indexPath` variable passed to us. We assign that entry to `_selectedEntry`. We then set the `_shouldStartEditing` variable to NO since this is not a brand new entry. Finally, we call `performSegueWithIdentifier:sender:` and pass it `ToFriendDetails` and nil as the parameters.

Now let's add the `prepareForSegue:sender:` method. We won't do anything in this method except add an `if` statement if the segue identifier is `ToFriendDetails`. This is just a stub right now, but we will update it after we get the `FriendDetailViewController` written.

```
#pragma mark - Navigation
- (void)prepareForSegue:(UIStoryboardSegue *)segue sender:(id)sender
{
    if([segue.identifier isEqualToString:@"ToFriendDetails"]){

    }
}
```

Next we need to add our delegate method for the `EntryCollectionViewCellDelegate`.

```
#pragma mark - EntryCollectionViewCellDelegate Methods
-(void)entryCollectionViewCell:(EntryCollectionViewCell *)cell longPressedForEntry:(NSString *)entry
{
    _selectedEntry = entry;
    UIAlertView *alert = [[UIAlertView alloc] initWithTitle:@"Delete Entry"
message:[NSString stringWithFormat:@"Are you sure you want to delete the entry for %@",entry]
delegate:self cancelButtonTitle:@"No" otherButtonTitles:@"Yes",nil];
    [alert setTag:1];
    [alert show];
}
```

On the first line we assign the entry that was passed to us to our _selectedEntry property. Then we instantiate an alert view that asks the user if they are sure they want to delete that entry. We set the tag on the alert to 1 because we will have other alerts later to deal with so we need to know which one this is. Finally we call show.

Because we are prompting the user with an alert and we want to know what they chose, we need to subscribe to the `UIAlertViewDelegate` as well. Select your `FriendsCollectionViewController.h` file and add `UIAlertViewDelegate` to the list of protocols we are subscribing to. The interface should now look like this:

```
@interface FriendsCollectionViewController : UICollectionViewController <UICollectionViewDataSource,
UICollectionViewDelegate, EntryCollectionViewCellDelegate, UIAlertViewDelegate>
```

Now let's add the `UIAlertViewDelegate` method `alertView:clickedButtonAtIndex:`.

```
#pragma mark - UIAlertViewDelegate Methods
-(void)alertView:(UIAlertView *)alertView clickedButtonAtIndex:(NSInteger)buttonIndex {
    if(alertView.tag == 1){
        if(buttonIndex == alertView.firstOtherButtonIndex)
            [self deleteEntry:_selectedEntry];

        _selectedEntry = nil;
    }
}
```

We start off by checking to see whether the tag for the `alertView` is in fact 1. If it is, we check to see whether the `buttonIndex` that was passed matched the index of the first other button index. If it is, which means they tapped on "Yes", then we call a new instance method `deleteEntry:` and pass it the _selectedEntry. Then we set _selectedEntry to nil. We haven't created the `deleteEntry:` method yet so let's create it now:

```
#pragma mark - Data Methods
-(void)deleteEntry:(NSString *)entry {
    [_entries removeObject:entry];
    [self.collectionView reloadData];
}
```

This is a pretty simple method. We just remove the object from our entries array and call `reloadData` on the `collectionView` so that our view refreshes. The final thing we need to do is add a method for our add button.

```
#pragma mark - Button Methods
-(IBAction)btnAddPressed:(id)sender {
    [_entries addObject:[NSString stringWithFormat:@"Friend %i",[_entries count] + 1]];
    [self.collectionView reloadData];
}
```

We do pretty much the same thing here as we did in delete entry except we add an object to the array instead of remove one. We use the `stringWithFormat:` method to create the string object by concatenating "Friend" with the total count of the array plus one.

Our final step is to go into the storyboard and change the class for our `UICollectionViewControl` and wire up our Bar Button.

1. Select `UICollectionViewController` in the `Main.storyboard`.

2. Change the class to `FriendsCollectionViewController`.

3. Ctrl-drag from the Bar Button item to the `FriendsCollectonViewController` and select `btnAddPressed:` under the Sent Actions heading in the popup.

FriendDetailViewController

Now we can lay the foundation for the `FriendsViewController`. Select the `FriendsViewController.h` file and let's get to work. We start by defining the protocol for our `FriendsCollectionViewControllerDelegate`. Add this line just above the `@interface` line.

```
@protocol FriendDetailViewControllerDelegate;
```

Next we subscribe to four delegate protocols that we use in the implementation file. They are `UITextFieldDelegate`, `UINavigationControllerDelegate`, `UIActionSheetDelegate`, and `UIImagePickerControllerDelegate`. One thing to note here is that we aren't actually calling any methods on the `UINavigationControllerDelegate`, but the `UIImagePickerControllerDelegate` does require that we subscribe to it because it will be using methods on our behalf.

```
@interface FriendDetailViewController : UIViewController <UITextFieldDelegate,
UINavigationControllerDelegate, UIActionSheetDelegate, UIImagePickerControllerDelegate>
```

Next we will define some public properties inside the interface:

```
@property (assign) id<FriendDetailViewControllerDelegate> delegate;
@property BOOL shouldStartEditing;
```

The last thing we need to do is define our actual delegate protocol. We will add a delegate method `detailViewControllerDidClose:` and we will pass this controller as its parameter.

```
@protocol FriendDetailViewControllerDelegate <NSObject>
-(void)detailViewControllerDidClose:(FriendDetailViewController *)detailViewController;
@end
```

Now we need to move over to our `FriendDetailViewController.m` file. The first thing we will do is add an import for the Quartz Core framework just above the `FriendDetailViewController.h` import. We are doing this because we want to define a border around our image using quartz core. We will also import the `UIImage+Resize.h` category to handle image resizing.

```
#import "UIImage+Resize.h"
#import <QuartzCore/QuartzCore.h>
```

We also need to create the properties that we will use to interact with the Text Fields and Image View that we created in the storyboard file.

```
@interface FriendDetailViewController ()
@property (weak) IBOutlet UITextField *txtFirstName;
@property (weak) IBOutlet UITextField *txtLastName;
@property (weak) IBOutlet UITextField *txtDisplayName;
@property (weak) IBOutlet UITextField *txtFavoriteNumber;
@property (weak) IBOutlet UIImageView *imgFriend;
@end
```

Next we will add an instance variable for the `UIImagePickerController`. Your `@implementation` line should now look like this.

```
@implementation FriendDetailViewController {
    UIImagePickerController *_picker;
}
```

We will now add 3 methods that we will use to configure our view.

```
-(void)disableAllFields {
    [_txtFirstName setEnabled:NO];
    [_txtLastName setEnabled:NO];
    [_txtDisplayName setEnabled:NO];
    [_txtFavoriteNumber setEnabled:NO];
    for(UIGestureRecognizer *gesture in [_imgFriend gestureRecognizers]){
        [_imgFriend removeGestureRecognizer:gesture];
    }
}

-(void)enableAllFields {
    [_txtFirstName setEnabled:YES];
    [_txtLastName setEnabled:YES];
    [_txtDisplayName setEnabled:YES];
    [_txtFavoriteNumber setEnabled:YES];
```

```
    UITapGestureRecognizer *tapGesture = [[UITapGestureRecognizer alloc] initWithTarget:self
action:@selector(photoTapped:)];
    [_imgFriend addGestureRecognizer:tapGesture];
}

- (void)configureView {
    _imgFriend.layer.borderColor = [UIColor darkGrayColor].CGColor;
    _imgFriend.layer.borderWidth = 2.0f;

    _imgFriend.image = [UIImage imageNamed:@"ImgNoImage"];
}
```

The first two methods are used to enable and disable the editing in the view. If we are in edit mode, we will add a tap gesture to the image view that calls the photoTapped: method when the image view is tapped. When we exit edit mode, we remove the tap gesture so that tapping has no effect.

Inside the configure view method we use quartz core to add a border to the image view. Then we assign our image asset, ImgNoImage, to the image view.

Next we need to add our photoTapped: method so that something actually happens when we tap the image.

```
-(void)photoTapped:(UIGestureRecognizer *)gesture {
    UIActionSheet *actionSheet = [[UIActionSheet alloc] initWithTitle:@"Change Photo" delegate:self
cancelButtonTitle:@"Cancel" destructiveButtonTitle:nil otherButtonTitles:@"Take Photo",@"Choose
From Library",nil];

    [actionSheet showFromTabBar:self.tabBarController.tabBar];
}
```

In this method we create a simple action sheet to ask the user if they want to take a photo with their camera or choose a photo from the photo library. We call the method showFromTabBar: because this view resides inside a UITabBarController.

Now we need to add a delegate method for the UIActionSheet called actionSheet:clickedButtonAtIndex:.

```
#pragma mark - UIActionSheetDelegate Methods
-(void)actionSheet:(UIActionSheet *)actionSheet clickedButtonAtIndex:(NSInteger)buttonIndex {
    if(_picker != nil){
        [_picker dismissViewControllerAnimated:NO completion:nil];
        _picker = nil;
    }

    switch (buttonIndex) {
        case 0: {
            _picker = [[UIImagePickerController alloc] init];
            [_picker setDelegate:self];
            [_picker setSourceType:UIImagePickerControllerSourceTypeCamera];
            [_picker setAllowsEditing:YES];

            [self presentViewController:_picker animated:YES completion:nil];
        }   break;
```

```
        case 1: {
            _picker = [[UIImagePickerController alloc] init];
            [_picker setDelegate:self];
            [_picker setSourceType:UIImagePickerControllerSourceTypePhotoLibrary];
            [_picker setAllowsEditing:YES];

            [self presentViewController:_picker animated:YES completion:nil];
        } break;
        default:
            break;
    }
}
```

The method starts off by checking to see whether _picker has been allocated. If it has, then we call the method dismissViewControllerAnimated:completion: to make sure the picker is not visible. Then we assign nil to it to clear it out completely.

We use a switch statement to determine what button the user pressed. If they pressed Take Photo, then that button's index is going to be 0 and if they pressed Choose From Library, it will be 1. Inside of each case we instantiate the UIImagePickerController, set its delegate to this view controller, set the source type to UIImagePickerControllerSourceTypeCamera or UIImagePickerControllerSourceTypePhotoLibrary depending on what button they pressed, and set allows editing to YES. We then call the method presentViewController:animated:completion: on our self to display the UIImagePickerController.

Now we need to add two UIImagePickerControllerDelegate methods.

```
#pragma mark - UIImagePickerControllerDelegate Methods
-(void)imagePickerControllerDidCancel:(UIImagePickerController *)picker {
    [self dismissViewControllerAnimated:YES completion:nil];
}

-(void)imagePickerController:(UIImagePickerController *)picker
didFinishPickingMediaWithInfo:(NSDictionary *)info {
    UIImage *image = (UIImage *)[info objectForKey:UIImagePickerControllerEditedImage];

    UIImage *resizedImage = [image resizedImage:CGSizeMake(560, 560)
interpolationQuality:kCGInterpolationHigh];
    [_imgFriend setImage:resizedImage];

    [self dismissViewControllerAnimated:YES completion:nil];
}
```

The first method, imagePickerControllerDidCancel: is called when the user cancels the image picker. The only thing we do here is dismiss the image picker, which brings the user back to our view.

The second method imagePickerController: didFinishPickingMediaWithInfo: is where we handle the image the user either took or selected. Because we enabled editing, the user will be creating a square image that we can access by using the constant UIImagePickerControllerEditedImage. We take that image and then resize it to 560 ×650 using the method resizeImage:interpolationQuality: that is provided in the UIImage+Resize Category on UIImage. Then we assign the image to the _imgFriend image view and dismiss our image picker.

Now we need to implement one of the UITextField delegate methods called textFieldShouldReturn:. You have already done this before so it should be familiar.

```
#pragma mark - UITextFieldDelegate Methods
-(BOOL)textFieldShouldReturn:(UITextField *)textField {
    if([textField isEqual:_txtFirstName]){
        [_txtLastName becomeFirstResponder];
    } else if([textField isEqual:_txtLastName]){
        if([_txtDisplayName.text isEqualToString:@""])
            _txtDisplayName.text =
[NSString stringWithFormat:@"%@ %@",_txtFirstName.text,_txtLastName.text];
        [_txtDisplayName becomeFirstResponder];
    } else if([textField isEqual:_txtDisplayName]){
        [_txtFavoriteNumber becomeFirstResponder];
    } else if([textField isEqual:_txtFavoriteNumber]){
        [_txtFavoriteNumber resignFirstResponder];
    }

    return YES;
}
```

Here we check the text field and move to the next text field similar to what we have done in the past. The only difference here is that right before we move to the _txtDisplayName field we check to see if it is empty. If it is, we autofill the display name with a concatenated value of the first name and second name.

Now we will add some Bar Button methods:

```
#pragma mark - Bar Button Methods
-(void)btnEditPressed:(id)sender {
    [self enableAllFields];
    UIBarButtonItem *doneButton = [[UIBarButtonItem alloc] initWithTitle:@"Done"
style:UIBarButtonItemStyleDone target:self action:@selector(btnDonePressed:)];
    [self.navigationItem setRightBarButtonItem:doneButton animated:YES];

    [self.navigationItem setLeftBarButtonItem:nil animated:YES];
}

-(void)btnDonePressed:(id)sender {
    [self disableAllFields];

    UIBarButtonItem *editButton = [[UIBarButtonItem alloc] initWithTitle:@"Edit"
style:UIBarButtonItemStyleBordered target:self action:@selector(btnEditPressed:)];
    [self.navigationItem setRightBarButtonItem:editButton animated:YES];

    UIBarButtonItem *backButton = [[UIBarButtonItem alloc] initWithTitle:@"Back"
style:UIBarButtonItemStyleBordered target:self action:@selector(btnBackPressed:)];
    [self.navigationItem setLeftBarButtonItem:backButton animated:YES];
}

-(void)btnBackPressed:(id)sender {
    [_delegate detailViewControllerDidClose:self];
}
```

The first method btnEditPressed: enables all the fields for editing by calling our enableAllFields method. Then we create a UIBarButtonItem titled "Done" and give it an action of btnDonePressed:. We replace the right Bar Button item with our Done button and remove the left Bar Button item. Removing the left Bar Button item makes sure that the user is not in an edit mode when they return to the collection view.

The second method is btnDonePressed:. We disable all the fields by calling our disableAllFields method. Then we set up the Bar Buttons back to their original state by creating an editButton and a Back button adding those to our navigation item.

The final method is btnBackPressed: and right now it only calls our delegate method detailViewControllerDidClose:.

The last thing we need to do is setup our viewDidLoad.

```
- (void)viewDidLoad
{
    [super viewDidLoad];

    UIBarButtonItem *editButton = [[UIBarButtonItem alloc] initWithTitle:@"Edit"
style:UIBarButtonItemStyleBordered target:self action:@selector(btnEditPressed:)];
    [self.navigationItem setRightBarButtonItem:editButton];

    UIBarButtonItem *backButton = [[UIBarButtonItem alloc] initWithTitle:@"Back"
style:UIBarButtonItemStyleBordered target:self action:@selector(btnBackPressed:)];
    [self.navigationItem setLeftBarButtonItem:backButton];
    [self.navigationItem setHidesBackButton:YES];

    [self configureView];
    [self disableAllFields];

    if(_shouldStartEditing) {
        [self btnEditPressed:nil];
        [_txtFirstName becomeFirstResponder];
    }
}
```

This should be self-explanatory by now. We create our bar buttons and assign them accordingly. We then call our configure view that sets our image border and applies our default image. We disable all the fields so that we aren't in edit mode. Then we check to see if we shouldStartEditing and if so, we simulate the Edit button being pressed by calling btnEditPressed:. Finally, we set the first text field to become the first responder so that it becomes selected and the keyboard shows.

The final thing we need to do is to set up our storyboard to interact with this file.

1.   Select the UIViewController in the storyboard and set its class to FriendDetailViewController.

2.   In the Connections Inspector drag a connection for imgFriend, txtDisplayName, txtFavoriteNumber, txtFirstName, and txtLastName to the appropriate object in the view.

3.   Next, Ctrl-drag from each of the text fields to the FriendDetailViewController object and select delegate underneath Outlets in the popup.

The final step is to go back and adjust the `FriendsCollectionViewController`. Open the `FriendsColl ectionViewController.h` file and add the import for the `FriendDetailViewController.h` file.

```
#import "FriendDetailViewController.h"
```

We also need to subscribe to the `FriendDetailViewControllerDelegate` Protocol. Your interface line should now look like this:

```
@interface FriendsCollectionViewController : UICollectionViewController <UICollectionViewDataSource,
UICollectionViewDelegate, EntryCollectionViewCellDelegate, UIAlertViewDelegate,
FriendDetailViewControllerDelegate>
```

Now we need to add the delegate method `detailViewControllerDidClose:`. The only thing we are doing right now is telling our navigation controller to go to the root controller by calling `popToRootViewControllerAnimated:`. We will do more with this method later.

```
#pragma mark - FriendDetailViewControllerDelegate Methods
-(void)detailViewControllerDidClose:(FriendDetailViewController *)detailViewController {
    [self.navigationController popToRootViewControllerAnimated:YES];
}
```

Finally, let's update our `prepareForSegue:sender` method so that it looks like this:

```
#pragma mark - Navigation
- (void)prepareForSegue:(UIStoryboardSegue *)segue sender:(id)sender
{
    if([segue.identifier isEqualToString:@"ToFriendDetails"]){
        [[segue destinationViewController] setDelegate:self];
        [[segue destinationViewController] setShouldStartEditing:_shouldStartEditing];
    }

}
```

Here we are just assigning our self as the delegate for the `FriendDetailViewController` and sending our `property _shouldStartEditing`. Remember this is the Boolean value that determines if we launch the view in edit more or if we are just viewing.

Go ahead and build and run the app. You should be able to add new Friends, delete them if you long press on them too. You can select an image in the detail view and it will show up in that view. None of this is being saved yet, but it lays the foundation for us to concentrate solely on integrating `UIDocument`.

UIDocument

`UIDocument` is an abstract base class that handles the managing of data and documents. Subclassing `UIDocument` gives you a lot of things right of the box such as:

- Asynchronous reading and writing of data on a background queue.

- Coordinated reading and writing of document files already integrated with iCloud.

- Support for conflict resolution.
- Safe saving of document data by writing a temporary file first and then overwriting the old document.
- Automatic saving of document data at opportune moments by the system.

What does this mean to you though? This means that you have to write less of the management code and can actually concentrate on your app and your document model. You won't have to waste any time and effort on writing or optimizing these tasks as Apple has already done that for you.

To subclass `UIDocument` you must implement two methods. Those are `contentsForType:error:` and `loadFromContents:ofType:error:`. These two methods handle the reading and writing of your document.

We will be using `UIDocument` to save a document package because we will be handling images and text with the use of `NSFileWrapper`. You could however save a data blob if your file was a singular piece of data, but overall it is not recommended. Packages are much more efficient for both the local file system and iCloud.

In this section we will create our object models, which will conform to the `NSCoding` protocol, as well as our `UIDocument` subclass. Once we have those created we will then go back to our test app and begin modifying our Collection View Controller, Collection View Cell, and Detail View Controller to handle our `UIDocument`. Let's get started.

Our Document Model

We start out by creating a data model for our documents metadata. Splitting up our document model in such a way allows us to be more efficient when viewing the documents we have before we decide to view one of them. Metadata is lightweight as compared to the actual data inside our document so it is passed around a lot quicker and uses less memory.

Let's create a new Objective-C class that is a subclass of `NSObject`. We will call this class `CTMetadata`. Now open the `CTMetadata.h` file. The first thing we want to do is subscribe to the NSCoding protocol. The NSCoding protocol declares the two methods that a class must implement so that instances of that class can be encoded and decoded. This capability provides the basis for archiving (where objects and other structures are stored on disk) and distribution (where objects are copied to different address spaces). Our interface line should now look like this:

```
@interface CTMetadata : NSObject <NSCoding>
```

We also need to add two public properties. One will be for our thumbnail, which is displayed in the CollectionViewCell and the other is our display name, which is also displayed in the CollectionViewCell.

```
@property (strong) UIImage *thumbnail;
@property (strong) NSString *displayName;
```

Moving over to the `CTMetadata.m` file we will create three local constants using defines. These should be just after the import statement, but before the `@implementation` line.

```objc
#define kVersionKey @"VERSION"
#define kThumbnailKey @"THUMBNAIL"
#define kDisplayNameKey @"DISPLAY_NAME"
```

Now we will create two init methods. The first being our full init method, which assigns values to the properties we created earlier on initialization and another that will call this method with nil values.

```objc
- (id)initWithThumbnail:(UIImage *)thumbnail andDisplayName:(NSString *)displayName{
    if((self = [super init])){
        _thumbnail = thumbnail;
        _displayName = displayName;
    }

    return self;
}

- (id)init {
    return [self initWithThumbnail:nil andDisplayName:nil];
}
```

The reason we have both these implementations is because when we create a document we won't have any data, but if we are decoding a metadata object we will have data. If this is confusing, the next methods should clear this up.

Now we need to implement our two NSCoding methods.

```objc
#pragma mark - NSCoding Methods
- (id)initWithCoder:(NSCoder *)aDecoder {
    NSInteger version = [aDecoder decodeIntForKey:kVersionKey];

    if(version == 1){
        NSData *thumbnailData = [aDecoder decodeObjectForKey:kThumbnailKey];
        UIImage *thumbnail = [UIImage imageWithData:thumbnailData];
        NSString *displayName = [aDecoder decodeObjectForKey:kDisplayNameKey];

        return [self initWithThumbnail:thumbnail andDisplayName:displayName];
    } else {
        return [self init];
    }
}

- (void)encodeWithCoder:(NSCoder *)aCoder {
    [aCoder encodeInt:1 forKey:kVersionKey];
    NSData *thumbnailData = UIImagePNGRepresentation(_thumbnail);
    [aCoder encodeObject:thumbnailData forKey:kThumbnailKey];
    [aCoder encodeObject:_displayName forKey:kDisplayNameKey];
}
```

Let's start with the encodeWithCoder: method because it is the writing portion. This method gets passed in an NSCoder object. We first use this object to encode and int value for the key kVersionKey. The value we are encoding is 1 since this is our first version of the file. It is recommended that you include a file type version with your UIDocuments so that down the line you have flexibility if you need to change your document model in future releases.

The next thing we do is convert our thumbnail data into an NSData object using UIImagePNGRepresentation(). Next we call encodeObject:forKey: twice on our NSCoder object. The first one is for our thumbnail data and the second is for our display name string.

Moving on to the initWithCoder: method, we also receive an NSCoder object as the parameter. Because this is our read method, we start out by calling the decodeIntForKey: method on our NSCoder with the key kVersionKey. Now that we have extracted the version number, we check to see if it is equal to 1. If it isn't, we just return a blank initialized CTMetadata object. If it is, we use the decodeObjectForKey: method to get our Image data and our display name. The image data then has to be converted to a UIImage object using the imageWithData: class method on UIImage. Finally we return our fully initialized CTMetadata object by calling initWithThumbnail:andDisplayName:.

That is all there is to our CTMetadata object. Now we need to create our actual data model. Let's create another new Objective-C class that is a subclass of NSObject and call it CTData. Just like we did with CTMetadata we want to subscribe to the NSCoding protocol. Then we will add some public properties.

```
@property (strong) NSString *firstName;
@property (strong) NSString *lastName;
@property (strong) NSString *displayName;
@property (strong) NSNumber *favoriteNumber;
@property (strong) UIImage *photo;
```

Now we can move on over to the CTData.m file. We will be doing the exact same thing that we did in the CTMetadata.m file. Here is what your .m file should look like when you are done:

```
#import "CTData.h"

#define kVersionKey @"VERSION"
#define kFirstNameKey @"FIRST_NAME"
#define kLastNameKey @"LAST_NAME"
#define kDisplayNameKey @"DISPLAY_NAME"
#define kFavoriteNumberKey @"FAVORITE_NUMBER"
#define kPhotoKey @"PHOTO"

@implementation CTData

- (id)initWithFirstName:(NSString *)firstName lastName:(NSString *)lastName displayName:(NSString *)
displayName favoriteNumber:(NSNumber *)favoriteNumber andPhoto:(UIImage *)photo {
    if((self = [super init])){
        _firstName = firstName;
        _lastName = lastName;
        _displayName = displayName;
        _favoriteNumber = favoriteNumber;
        _photo = photo;
    }

    return self;
}
```

```objectivec
- (id)init {
    return [self initWithFirstName:nil lastName:nil displayName:nil favoriteNumber:nil
andPhoto:nil];
}

#pragma mark - NSCoding Methods
- (id)initWithCoder:(NSCoder *)aDecoder {
    NSInteger version = [aDecoder decodeIntForKey:kVersionKey];

    if(version == 1){
        NSString *firstName = [aDecoder decodeObjectForKey:kFirstNameKey];
        NSString *lastName = [aDecoder decodeObjectForKey:kLastNameKey];
        NSString *displayName = [aDecoder decodeObjectForKey:kDisplayNameKey];
        NSNumber *favoriteNumber = [aDecoder decodeObjectForKey:kFavoriteNumberKey];

        NSData *photoData = [aDecoder decodeObjectForKey:kPhotoKey];
        UIImage *photo = [UIImage imageWithData:photoData];

        return [self initWithFirstName:firstName lastName:lastName displayName:displayName
favoriteNumber:favoriteNumber andPhoto:photo];
    } else {
        return [self init];
    }
}

- (void)encodeWithCoder:(NSCoder *)aCoder {
    [aCoder encodeInt:1 forKey:kVersionKey];
    [aCoder encodeObject:_firstName forKey:kFirstNameKey];
    [aCoder encodeObject:_lastName forKey:kLastNameKey];
    [aCoder encodeObject:_displayName forKey:kDisplayNameKey];
    [aCoder encodeObject:_favoriteNumber forKey:kFavoriteNumberKey];

    NSData *photoData = UIImagePNGRepresentation(_photo);
    [aCoder encodeObject:photoData forKey:kPhotoKey];
}

@end
```

Now that we have the data model out of the way we can bring it all into a UIDocument subclass.

CTDocument

Create a new Objective-C class that is a subclass of UIDocument and call it CTDocument. In the preceding CTDocument.h file the @interface line we need to add a class declaration for CTData and CTMetadata.

```objectivec
@class CTData;
@class CTMetadata;
```

Next we will create a define that will be used for our file extension. We put this in this class because it related specifically to this document rather than our entire project.

```
#define CT_EXTENSION @"ict"
```

Inside our interface we will create one public property for accessing our metadata, because our metadata will actually be created by values from the data model on save this is safe.

```
@property (strong, nonatomic) CTMetadata *metadata;
```

We will then create a setter and getter method for each of our data properties. We do this because we want to intercept all these calls rather than let the app access these properties directly.

```
-(NSString *)firstName;
-(void)setFirstName:(NSString *)firstName;
-(NSString *)lastName;
-(void)setLastName:(NSString *)lastName;
-(NSString *)displayName;
-(void)setDisplayName:(NSString *)displayName;
-(NSNumber *)favoriteNumber;
-(void)setFavoriteNumber:(NSNumber *)favoriteNumber;
-(UIImage *)photo;
-(void)setPhoto:(UIImage *)photo;
-(NSString *)description;
```

Now let's move on to our CTDocument.m file. First, we need to add some imports. Add these above the CTDocument.h import.

```
#import "UIImage+Resize.h"
#import "CTData.h"
#import "CTMetadata.h"
```

Next, we will add two local constants that we will use in our implementation.

```
#define kDataKey @"ctdocument.data"
#define kMetadataKey @"ctdocument.metadata"
```

Now we need to create a private interface that will hold our CTData property and our NSFileWrapper property.

```
@interface CTDocument()
@property (strong, nonatomic) CTData *data;
@property (strong, nonatomic) NSFileWrapper *fileWrapper;
@end
```

Inside our implementation we need to first implement the writing method for UIDocument, which is contentsForType:error:. To do this we will add a second method called encodeObject:toWrappers: withFilename:

```
#pragma mark - Document Writing Methods
- (id)contentsForType:(NSString *)typeName error:(NSError *__autoreleasing *)outError {
    if(self.metadata == nil || self.data == nil)
        return nil;

    NSMutableDictionary *wrappers = [NSMutableDictionary dictionary];
    [self encodeObject:_data toWrappers:wrappers withKey:kDataKey];
    [self encodeObject:_metadata toWrappers:wrappers withKey:kMetadataKey];

    NSFileWrapper *fileWrapper = [[NSFileWrapper alloc] initDirectoryWithFileWrappers:wrappers];

    return fileWrapper;
}

- (void)encodeObject:(id<NSCoding>)object toWrappers:(NSMutableDictionary *)wrappers
withKey:(NSString *)key {
    @autoreleasepool {
        NSMutableData *data = [NSMutableData data];
        NSKeyedArchiver *archiver = [[NSKeyedArchiver alloc] initForWritingWithMutableData:data];
        [archiver encodeObject:object forKey:@"DATA"];
        [archiver finishEncoding];

        NSFileWrapper *wrapper = [[NSFileWrapper alloc] initRegularFileWithContents:data];
        [wrappers setObject:wrapper forKey:key];
    }
}
```

Let's talk about encodeObject:toWrappers:withFilename: first. This method is passed three parameters. The first is our object that conforms to the NSCoding protocol, which is going to be NSData or NSMetadata. The second parameter is an NSMutableDictionary that we use to hold each NSFileWrapper that contains the encoded data. The final parameter is the key used as the NSFileWrapper key for the encoded object. We surround our actions in this method with an autoreleasepool so that the pool isn't drained until we utilize the NSMutableDictionary in the calling method.

We start by creating an NSMutableData object called data. We then create an NSKeyedArchiver by calling alloc and initForWritingWithMutableData: and passing our data object. We then call the method encodeObject:forKey on the archiver. This takes our passed in object and encodes it. We then wrap up the NSKeyedArchiver by calling finishEncoding.

The final step is to create an NSFileWrapper using alloc and initRegularFileWithContents: and passing it our data object that has been encoded. Then we add our wrapper to the passed in wrappers mutable dictionary using the key we passed into the object.

Looking at contentsForType:error: you can see that we first check to see if metadata or data are empty. By calling self.metadata and self.data, we utilize an accessor method that we will create later to be able to lazily load our data. If either of these is nil, then we return out of this method.

Now that we know we have data and metadata we create an NSMutableDictionary called wrappers that we will use in the following lines. We then call encodeObject:toWrappers:withKey: for both our data and metadata passing the respective key. Finally, we create an NSFileWrapper and instantiate it with our wrappers dictionary by calling initDirectoryWithFileWrappers:. Then we return our file wrapper.

Next we will add the data reading methods:

```
#pragma mark - Document Reading Methods
-(BOOL)loadFromContents:(id)contents ofType:(NSString *)typeName error:(NSError *__autoreleasing *)
outError {
    _fileWrapper = (NSFileWrapper *)contents;

    _data = nil;
    _metadata = nil;

    return YES;
}


- (id)decodeObjectFromWrapperWithKey:(NSString *)key {
    NSFileWrapper *fileWrapper = [_fileWrapper.fileWrappers objectForKey:key];
    if(!fileWrapper)
        return nil;

    NSData *data = [fileWrapper regularFileContents];
    NSKeyedUnarchiver *unarchiver = [[NSKeyedUnarchiver alloc] initForReadingWithData:data];

    return [unarchiver decodeObjectForKey:@"DATA"];
}
```

Starting with loadFromContents:ofType:error: we take the contents parameter, which is an NSFileWrapper, and assign it to our local NSFileWrapper property. We use this later to lazily load our metadata and data. Next we set our _data and _metadata objects to nil also because we will lazily load them when needed. Finally, we return YES to tell the system there was no problem loading the document.

The next method decodeObjectFromWrapperWithKey: simply grabs the fileWrapper for the specific object using the passed in key. If it was unable to obtain a fileWrapper, it returns nil and ends execution. With the retrieved fileWrapper we fetch the NSData object by using the regularFileContents method against NSFileWrapper. We then create an NSKeyedUnarchiver by calling alloc and initForReadingWithData: passing in the data we just fetched from the file wrapper. Finally we call decodeObjectForKey: against our unarchiver and pass in our global key name @"DATA" that we used earlier in the writing section. This unarchived data is returned.

I have used the term lazily load multiple times and now is the time that it should all come together. We will create two accessor methods. Once for CTData and one for CTMetadata.

```
#pragma mark - Property Accessors
-(CTData *)data {
    if(_data == nil){
        if(_fileWrapper != nil)
            _data = [self decodeObjectFromWrapperWithKey:kDataKey];
```

```
        else
            _data = [[CTData alloc] init];
    }

    return _data;
}

-(CTMetadata *)metadata {
    if(_metadata == nil){
        if(_fileWrapper != nil)
            _metadata = [self decodeObjectFromWrapperWithKey:kMetadataKey];
        else
            _metadata = [[CTMetadata alloc] init];
    }

    return _metadata;
}
```

Both of these methods are identical except that we are working with CTData in one and CTMetadata in the other. With that being said, let's just walk through the first one for CTData.

When [self data] or self.data is called, this method will be called. It first checks to see whether _data is equal to nil. If it isn't, then we just pass back our _data object. If it is nil, then we check to see if our NSFileWrapper property has been set. If it has, we use it to call decodeObjectFromWrapperWithKey: passing in our constant kDataKey. If it hasn't, we initialize a blank CTData object.

We can think of the process like this. When we first access a saved document, we have a file wrapper. Therefore, we can decode it with that filewrapper, which in turn gives us our instantiated CTData object. However, when we create a brand new document we have decoded anything so we will create blank CTData and CTMetadata objects instead.

Now we need to add all our public access methods that we added in our interface.

```
-(NSString *)firstName {
    return [self.data firstName];
}

-(void)setFirstName:(NSString *)firstName {
    if([[self.data firstName] isEqualToString:firstName])
        return;

    NSString *oldFirstName = [self.data firstName];
    [self.data setFirstName:firstName];

    [self.undoManager setActionName:@"First Name Change"];
    [self.undoManager registerUndoWithTarget:self selector:@selector(setFirstName:)
object:oldFirstName];
}

-(NSString *)lastName {
    return [self.data lastName];
}
```

```objc
-(void)setLastName:(NSString *)lastName {
    if([[self.data lastName] isEqualToString:lastName])
        return;

    NSString *oldLastName = [self.data lastName];
    [self.data setLastName:lastName];

    [self.undoManager setActionName:@"Last Name Change"];
    [self.undoManager registerUndoWithTarget:self selector:@selector(setLastName:)
object:oldLastName];
}

-(NSString *)displayName {
    return [self.data displayName];
}

-(void)setDisplayName:(NSString *)displayName {
    if([[self.data displayName] isEqualToString:displayName])
        return;

    NSString *oldDisplayName = [self.data displayName];
    [self.data setDisplayName:displayName];
    [self.metadata setDisplayName:displayName];

    [self.undoManager setActionName:@"Display Name Change"];
    [self.undoManager registerUndoWithTarget:self selector:@selector(setDisplayName:)
object:oldDisplayName];
}

-(NSNumber *)favoriteNumber {
    return [self.data favoriteNumber];
}

-(void)setFavoriteNumber:(NSNumber *)favoriteNumber {
    if([[self.data favoriteNumber] isEqualToNumber:favoriteNumber])
        return;

    NSNumber *oldFavoriteNumber = [self.data favoriteNumber];
    [self.data setFavoriteNumber:favoriteNumber];

    [self.undoManager setActionName:@"Favorite Number Change"];
    [self.undoManager registerUndoWithTarget:self selector:@selector(setFavoriteNumber:)
object:oldFavoriteNumber];
}

-(UIImage *)photo {
    return [self.data photo];
}
```

```objc
-(void)setPhoto:(UIImage *)photo {
    if([[self.data photo] isEqual:photo])
        return;

    UIImage *oldPhoto = [self.data photo];
    [self.data setPhoto:photo];
    [self.metadata setThumbnail:[photo resizedImage:CGSizeMake(280, 280)
interpolationQuality:kCGInterpolationHigh]];

    [self.undoManager setActionName:@"Photo Change"];
    [self.undoManager registerUndoWithTarget:self selector:@selector(setPhoto:) object:oldPhoto];
}

-(NSString *)description {
    return [[self.fileURL lastPathComponent] stringByDeletingPathExtension];
}
```

As you can see in each of our getter methods we access the property by calling `self.data`. This is another mechanism of the lazy loading. It ensures that we have a data object and if we haven't accessed the data object before it will cause it to be either decoded or instantiated as a blank object.

The setter methods are a little different so we should go into more detail with these. We start off by checking to see if the value is equal to the value we are passing in. If it is then we return out. This keeps us from writing the same values over and over thus keeping our app performance efficient and not inadvertently signaling system writes when no data has actually changed. So, if the value is different, then we copy the old value into a variable that we will use with the undo manager (more on that in a second). Then we set the property to the new value.

The next two methods work with the NSUndoManager. We start by calling the method `setActionName:` and pass it a readable string for the action we are currently performing. We then call a second method on NSUndoManager called `registerUndoWithTarget:selector:object:`. Our target is naturally our self. For selector we pass in the selector that is currently performing the action. And for the object we pass in the copy of the object, or the old value. What this does is tell the undo manager that in order to undo what we just did we would want to call the `setSomething` method on our self and pass it the old value.

Now, we won't actually use this functionality in our app, but I wanted to show you how easy it is to implement. You can undo the last action by calling `[self.undoManager undo]`. You can do something similar for redo.

The final thing in these accessor methods to notice is both in our `setDisplayName` and `setPhoto:` methods. Because our metadata is derived from our data, we also set our metadata in these two places. In `setDisplayName` we just apply the value to both the data and metadata. However, in our `setPhoto` method we resize our image to create a thumbnail and set that image as our thumbnail property in metadata.

Now that we have created our document model and our document, we have one last class to create to make display our document previews a little easier.

Create a new Objective-C class that is a subclass of NSObject and name it CTEntry. Because this class is really only going to be handling the metadata we will want to add a class declaration for CTMetadata.

```
@class CTMetadata;
```

Next we will add some public properties:

```
@property (strong) NSURL *fileURL;
@property (strong) CTMetadata *metadata;
@property (assign) UIDocumentState state;
@property (strong) NSFileVersion *version;
```

And finally we will add an initialization method that will handle setting these properties for us:

```
-(id)initWithFileURL:(NSURL *)fileURL metadata:(CTMetadata *)metadata state:(UIDocumentState)state
andVersion:(NSFileVersion *)version;
```

Now, let's move into the CTEntry.m file and add the initializer and set all of our properties to those passed to it:

```
-(id)initWithFileURL:(NSURL *)fileURL metadata:(CTMetadata *)metadata state:(UIDocumentState)state
andVersion:(NSFileVersion *)version {
    if((self = [super init])){
        _fileURL = fileURL;
        _metadata = metadata;
        _state = state;
        _version = version;
    }

    return self;
}
```

That wraps up our UIDocument setup. Now we need to move on and modify our code to use our CTDocument instead of our generic NSString that we've been using so far.

Implementing CTDocument

Let's start by adding some imports to our FriendsCollectionViewController.m file:

```
#import "CTEntry.h"
#import "CTDocument.h"
#import "CTMetadata.h"
```

Now we need to add a property for the selectedDocument and adjust our selectedEntry to type CTEntry:

```
@property (strong) CTDocument *selectedDocument;
@property (strong) CTEntry *selectedEntry;
```

Next we need to modify our viewDidLoad so that we can initialize our entries NSMutableArray and call a new method that we will create shortly:

```
- (void)viewDidLoad
{
    [super viewDidLoad];

    _entries = [NSMutableArray array];
    [self reload];
}
```

Now, just above your UICollectionViewDatasource methods we need to create this reload method. It is very simple. We will remove all the objects from our entries array and call another method called loadLocal that we haven't created yet.

```
-(void)reload {
    [_entries removeAllObjects];
    [self loadLocal];
}
```

In the section we created called Data Methods we need to create our loadLocal method:

```
-(void)loadLocal {
    NSArray *localDocuments = [[NSFileManager defaultManager] contentsOfDirectoryAtURL:[AppDelegate
applicationDocumentsDirectory] includingPropertiesForKeys:nil options:0 error:nil];

    [localDocuments enumerateObjectsUsingBlock:^(NSURL *fileURL, NSUInteger idx, BOOL *stop) {
        if([[fileURL pathExtension] isEqualToString:CT_EXTENSION]){
            [self loadDocumentAtFileURL:fileURL];
        }
    }];

    [self.navigationItem.rightBarButtonItem setEnabled:YES];
}
```

The first line in this method gets an array of URLs inside our application's documents directory by calling contentsOfDirectoryAtURL:includingPropertiesForKeys:options:error:. We then use the enumeration method enumerateObjectsUsingBlock: on our NSArray to loop through the URLs. We compare the extension of each URL with the file extension that we defined in our CTDocument header file. If the NSURL has our document extension we call the method loadDocumentAtFileURL: and pass it the file URL. Let's write that method now.

```
-(void)loadDocumentAtFileURL:(NSURL *)fileURL {
    CTDocument *document = [[CTDocument alloc] initWithFileURL:fileURL];
    [document openWithCompletionHandler:^(BOOL success) {
        if(!success){
            NSLog(@"Unable to open document at %@",fileURL);
            return;
        }
```

```
            CTMetadata *metadata = [document metadata];
            NSURL *fileURL = [document fileURL];
            UIDocumentState state = [document documentState];
            NSFileVersion *version = [NSFileVersion currentVersionOfItemAtURL:fileURL];
            NSLog(@"Loaded file %@",[document fileURL]);

            [document closeWithCompletionHandler:^(BOOL success) {
                if(!success){
                    NSLog(@"There was an error closing the document at %@",fileURL);
                }

                dispatch_async(dispatch_get_main_queue(), ^{
                    [self addOrUpdateEntryWithURL:fileURL metadata:metadata state:state version:version];
                });
            }];
        }];
}
```

The first line allocates a CTDocument and calls the method initWithFileURL:. This is a method that is provided by the UIDocument sub class. Now that we have the document object we need to open it. This is done by calling the openWithCompletionHandler: method on our CTDocument. This method is also provided by the UIDocument subclass.

We first check for success. If we are unsuccessful, then we return out of the method. If we are successful, we create a CTMetadata object by assigning the metadata object from the document to our local metadata object. We grab the NSURL of the document, the document state, and the file version of the document as well. We then close the document because all we need is the metadata at this time.

It is important to remember that any document you open must be closed before it can be opened again. Be very careful to make sure you always close your documents when you are done with them.

We close the document by calling closeWithCompletionHandler:. We also check for success in this method although even if it fails we still want to carry on with the rest of the method. Next we call addOrUpdateEntryWithURL:metadata:state:version: on the main thread by calling it inside a dispatch_async black and passing it the dispatch_get_main_queue() parameter. Now let's write our method addOrUpdateEntryWithURL:metadata:state:version:.

```
-(void)addOrUpdateEntryWithURL:(NSURL *)fileURL metadata:(CTMetadata *)metadata
state:(UIDocumentState)state version:(NSFileVersion *)version {
    NSInteger index = [self indexOfEntryWithFileURL:fileURL];

    if(index == NSNotFound){
        CTEntry *entry = [[CTEntry alloc] initWithFileURL:fileURL metadata:metadata state:state
andVersion:version];

        [_entries addObject:entry];
        [_entries sortUsingComparator:^NSComparisonResult(CTEntry *entry1, CTEntry *entry2) {
            NSComparisonResult result = [[[entry1 metadata] displayName]
compare:[[entry2 metadata] displayName]];
            NSLog(@"results is %d",result);
            return result;
        }];
```

```
        index = [self indexOfEntryWithFileURL:fileURL];
        [self.collectionView insertItemsAtIndexPaths:@[[NSIndexPath indexPathForRow:index inSection:0]]];
    } else {
        CTEntry *entry = [_entries objectAtIndex:index];
        [entry setMetadata:metadata];
        [entry setState:state];
        [entry setVersion:version];

        [_entries sortUsingComparator:^NSComparisonResult(CTEntry *entry1, CTEntry *entry2) {
            NSComparisonResult result = [[[entry1 metadata] displayName]
compare:[[entry2 metadata] displayName]];
            NSLog(@"results is %d",result);
            return result;
        }];

        NSInteger newIndex = [self indexOfEntryWithFileURL:fileURL];
        if(index != newIndex){
            [self.collectionView moveItemAtIndexPath:[NSIndexPath indexPathForRow:index inSection:0]
toIndexPath:[NSIndexPath indexPathForRow:newIndex inSection:0]];
        }
        [self.collectionView reloadItemsAtIndexPaths:@[[NSIndexPath indexPathForRow:newIndex
inSection:0]]];
    }
}
```

We start off by finding the index of the CTEntry with the fileURL by calling indexOfEntryWithFileURL:. This is a helper method that we will write shortly. If the index is equal to NSNotFound, then we know that this item does not exist in the entries array so it is a new document.

If it is a new document, we create a new CTEntry by calling initWithFileURL:metadata:stat e:andVersion:. Then we add the new entry to our entries array. We then call an array method sortUsingComparator:. Inside the comparator block we compare the display names of each object and return the NSComparisonResult. We end up with an alphabetically sorted array. Because we sorted the array, we call the indexOfEntryWithFileURL: method again to determine our current index. Now that we know exactly where this new object is we call insertItemsAtIndexPaths: on our Collection View. This adds the object to our view.

If we are referencing a current document, we get the CTEntry by assigning what is at the given index in our entries array. We set the metadata, state, and version of the CTEntry to make sure it is current. We then perform a sort exactly like we did earlier to alphabetize the array. Next we set a newIndex variable by calling indexOfEntryWithFileURL:. Now that we have a new index we check to see whether our newIndex and index are not the same. If they aren't, then we now that we need to move our object. We do this by calling moveItemAtIndexPath:toIndexPath: against our Collection View. Finally, we call the method reloadItemsAtIndexPaths: and pass it an array with our single index path.

Now let's add our helper method indexOfEntryWithFileURL:.

```
-(NSInteger)indexOfEntryWithFileURL:(NSURL *)fileURL {
    __block NSInteger index = NSNotFound;
```

```
[_entries enumerateObjectsUsingBlock:^(CTEntry *entry, NSUInteger idx, BOOL *stop) {
    if([[entry fileURL] isEqual:fileURL]){
        index = idx;
        *stop = YES;
    }
}];


    return index;
}
```

As you can see, this method is very simple. We start off by setting our index to NSNotFound. Then we enumerate through our entries using the method enumerateObjectsUsingBlock:. We compare our fileURL with the entry fileURL. If they are equal, we set the index and tell the enumeration to stop. Finally, we return the index. Simple and sweet.

Now let's modify a few methods that we created earlier. Let's start with collectionView:cellForItemAt IndexPath:. We need to change the line where we get the entry and assign it to a type NSString and now assign it to a type CTEntry.

```
CTEntry *entry = _entries[indexPath.row];
```

Now in our collectionView:didSelectItemAtIndexPath: we need to change it to look like this.

```
- (void)collectionView:(UICollectionView *)collectionView didSelectItemAtIndexPath:(NSIndexPath *)
indexPath {
    CTEntry *entry = _entries[indexPath.row];

    _selectedDocument = [[CTDocument alloc] initWithFileURL:[entry fileURL]];
    _shouldStartEditing = NO;
    [_selectedDocument openWithCompletionHandler:^(BOOL success) {
        dispatch_async(dispatch_get_main_queue(), ^{
            [self performSegueWithIdentifier:@"ToFriendDetails" sender:nil];
        });
    }];
}
```

The first thing we do is change the type of entry to CTEntry. Then we initialize a CTDocument with the fileURL from our entry and assign it to selectedDocument. Because this file already exists, we set shouldStartEditing to NO. Then we call the method openWithCompletionHandler: on our selectedDocument. This method is handled on a background thread so when it is complete we call our performSegueWithIdentifier: method inside a dispatch_async call passing it the dispatch_get_main_queue() method as the queue parameter.

Now we need to modify our deleteEntry: method to look like the following:

```
-(void)deleteEntry:(CTEntry *)entry {
    NSFileManager *fileManager = [[NSFileManager alloc] init];
    [fileManager removeItemAtURL:[entry fileURL] error:nil];

    [self removeEntryWithURL:[entry fileURL]];
}
```

We start by changing the parameter type from NSString to CTEntry. Then we delete everything we had inside the method and start from scratch. We instantiate an NSFileManager object by calling alloc and init. Then we call the removeItemAtURL:error: method and pass it the fileURL from the passed in CTEntry. Finally, we call a method that we haven't created yet called removeEntryWithURL:. Let's write that method now.

```
-(void)removeEntryWithURL:(NSURL *)fileURL {
    NSInteger index = [self indexOfEntryWithFileURL:fileURL];

    [_entries removeObjectAtIndex:index];
    [self.collectionView deleteItemsAtIndexPaths:@[[NSIndexPath indexPathForRow:index
inSection:0]]];
}
```

We start by getting the index for the entry with the passed in fileURL by calling indexOfEntryWithFileURL:. Then we call the removeObjectAtIndex: method on our NSMutableArray to remove the entry. Finally, we call deleteItemsAtIndexPaths: and pass it an array with a single item which is the NSIndexPath of our object. This causes the UI to be updated without change.

We should also go into our btnAddPressed: and make our changes to create a CTDocument. The new method look like this:

```
-(IBAction)btnAddPressed:(id)sender {
    NSURL *fileURL = [self getDocmentURL:[self getDocumentFilename:@"Friend" forLocal:YES]];

    CTDocument *document = [[CTDocument alloc] initWithFileURL:fileURL];
    _shouldStartEditing = YES;
    [document saveToURL:[document fileURL] forSaveOperation:UIDocumentSaveForCreating
completionHandler:^(BOOL success) {
        if(!success)
            NSLog(@"There was an error saving the document - %@",fileURL);

        NSLog(@"File created at %@", fileURL);

        CTMetadata *metadata = [document metadata];
        NSURL *fileURL = [document fileURL];
        UIDocumentState state = [document documentState];
        NSFileVersion *version = [NSFileVersion currentVersionOfItemAtURL:fileURL];

        _selectedDocument = document;
        dispatch_async(dispatch_get_main_queue(), ^{
            [self addOrUpdateEntryWithURL:fileURL metadata:metadata state:state version:version];
            [self performSegueWithIdentifier:@"ToFriendDetails" sender:nil];
        });
    }];
}
```

We start by getting the fileURL. This is done by calling two new methods that we will create shortly. The first is getDocumentURL: and the second is getDocumentFilename:forLocal:. Once we have our fileURL we create a CTDocument by calling alloc and initWithFileURL:. Then we set our _shouldStartEditing property to YES because this is a brand new document.

Next we call saveToURL:forSaveOperation:completionHandler: on our document object. We then create a metadata object and assign the contents of our document's metadata to it. Then we create three more objects for fileURL, state, and version. I'm sure this looks familiar. Next we set our selectedDocument to the document we just created. Then we add a dispatch_async block to execute the next two calls on the main thread. The first method call we make is to ad dOrUpdateEntryWithURL:metadata:state:version, which creates a CTEntry for this document. Then we call performSeguqWithIdentifier and pass it "ToFriendDetails", which moves us to our FriendDetailViewController.

Now we can add those two methods that we referenced earlier.

```
-(NSURL *)getDocmentURL:(NSString *)filename {
    return [[AppDelegate applicationDocumentsDirectory] URLByAppendingPathComponent:filename
isDirectory:NO];
}

-(NSString *)getDocumentFilename:(NSString *)filename forLocal:(BOOL)isLocal {
    NSInteger docCount = 0;
    NSString *newDocName = nil;

    BOOL done = NO;
    BOOL first = YES;
    while(!done){
        if(first){
            first = NO;
            newDocName = [NSString stringWithFormat:@"%@.%@",filename,CT_EXTENSION];
        } else {
            newDocName = [NSString stringWithFormat:@"%@_%d.%@",filename,docCount,CT_EXTENSION];
        }

        BOOL nameExists = NO;
        if(isLocal){
            nameExists = [self documentNameExistsInObjects:newDocName];
        }

        if(!nameExists){
            break;
        } else {
            docCount++;
        }
    }

    return newDocName;
}
```

The first method getDocumentURL: currently just returns us the URL for the application documents directory. This method is more useful when we start integrating iCloud.

The second method is getDocumentFilename:forLocal:. The majority of the code in this method is within the while loop. The first time through the while loop we create the document name by using the passed in NSString parameter and adding our file extension to it. We then check to see if the name exists by calling the documentNameExistsInObjects: method. We will write this shortly.

If it does then nameExists is set to true and we break the while loop and return this new document name. If it does exist, we loop again, but this time adding a counter to the end of the filename. The same check is done until we find a unique name.

Now let's add the documentNameExistsInObjects: method:

```
-(BOOL)documentNameExistsInObjects:(NSString *)documentName {
    __block BOOL nameExists = NO;
    [_entries enumerateObjectsUsingBlock:^(CTEntry *entry, NSUInteger idx, BOOL *stop) {
        if([[[entry fileURL] lastPathComponent] isEqualToString:documentName]){
            nameExists = YES;
            *stop = YES;
        }
    }];

    return nameExists;
}
```

In this method we do a simple enumeration over our entries array and check the lastPathComponent(filename) and determine if any of them are equal to our passed in document name. If they are, we set the BOOL value for nameExists to YES and exit the enumeration. We return our BOOL value to let the receiver know our results.

The last thing we need to do in this file is modify our EntryCollectionViewCellDelegate method to take in a CTEntry instead of an NSString. We will modify the EntryCollectionViewCell next.

```
-(void)entryCollectionViewCell:(EntryCollectionViewCell *)cell longPressedForEntry:(CTEntry *)entry {
```

Now we need to go back and modify our EntryCollectionViewCell to handle our CTEntry object instead of the generic NSString we were using before. Open up the EntryCollectionViewCell.h file. We need to add the class declaration for CTEntry above our first protocol statement.

```
@class CTEntry;
```

Next we need to change the entry type in our configureCellForEntry:withDelegate method to use a CTEntry instead of NSString.

```
-(void)configureCellForEntry:(CTEntry *)entry
withDelegate:(id<EntryCollectionViewCellDelegate>)delegate;
```

The last change we need to make to this header file is to change the delegate method's final parameter from an NSString to a CTEntry.

```
-(void)entryCollectionViewCell:(EntryCollectionViewCell *)cell longPressedForEntry:(CTEntry *)entry;
```

Moving over to the EntryCollectionViewCell.m file we need to add an import statement for CTEntry.h and CTMetadata.h.

```
#import "CTEntry.h"
#import "CTMetadata.h"
```

Next we need to change our entry property type from NSString to CTEntry.

```
@property (assign) CTEntry *entry;
```

The last thing we need to do is change our configureCellForEntry:withDelegate method to first take a CTEntry as the first parameter instead of NSString. We also want to change the implementation to reflect the use of the CTEntry object.

```
-(void)configureCellForEntry:(CTEntry *)entry withDelegate:(id<EntryCollectionViewCellDelegate>)
delegate {
    if(entry == nil)
        return;

    _entry = entry;
    _delegate = delegate;

    if([[_entry metadata] thumbnail])
        _imgPhoto.image = [[_entry metadata] thumbnail];
    else
        _imgPhoto.image = [UIImage imageNamed:@"ImgCellNoImage"];

    _lblDisplayName.text = [[_entry metadata] displayName];
}
```

The main difference here is that we are peeking into the metadata object inside our entry object to get the thumbnail and the display name.

We are almost done implementing our CTDocument. The last thing we need to do is modify our FriendDetailViewController so that we can view and edit the document. Open up FriendDetailViewController.h and add the class declaration for CTDocument:

```
@class CTDocument;
```

Now let's add another property for a CTDocument:

```
@property (strong, nonatomic) CTDocument *document;
```

Moving over to FriendDetailViewController.m we need to add an import statement for CTDocument.h.

```
#import "CTDocument.h"
```

Next we need to modify configureView to now look like this:

```
- (void)configureView {
    _txtFirstName.text = [_document firstName];
    _txtLastName.text = [_document lastName];
    _txtDisplayName.text = [_document displayName];
    _txtFavoriteNumber.text = [[_document favoriteNumber] stringValue];
```

```
_imgFriend.layer.borderColor = [UIColor darkGrayColor].CGColor;
_imgFriend.layer.borderWidth = 2.0f;

if([_document photo])
    _imgFriend.image = [_document photo];
else
    _imgFriend.image = [UIImage imageNamed:@"ImgNoImage"];

}
```

Here we are just setting up our textfields to the values inside the document and setting our photo to the correct photo.

Our btnDone: method needs to be modified as well so that we can capture our new values from the textfields. Add the following just below the disableAllFields call and above the creation of the UIBarButtonItems.

```
[_document setFirstName:_txtFirstName.text];
    [_document setLastName:_txtLastName.text];
    [_document setDisplayName:_txtDisplayName.text];
    [_document setFavoriteNumber:[NSNumber numberWithFloat:[_txtFavoriteNumber.text floatValue]]];
```

Let's modify our image picker delegate method so that we now set the photo on the document when we have selected an image. It should now look like this.

```
-(void)imagePickerController:(UIImagePickerController *)picker
didFinishPickingMediaWithInfo:(NSDictionary *)info {
    UIImage *image = (UIImage *)[info objectForKey:UIImagePickerControllerEditedImage];

    UIImage *resizedImage = [image resizedImage:CGSizeMake(560, 560)
interpolationQuality:kCGInterpolationHigh];
    [_document setPhoto:resizedImage];
    [_imgFriend setImage:resizedImage];

    [self dismissViewControllerAnimated:YES completion:nil];
}
```

The last thing we want to do is modify our btnBackPressed: method so that it will close the document. Remember that we opened the document before we passed it to the view controller so we want to make sure and close it before we go back.

```
-(void)btnBackPressed:(id)sender {
    [_document saveToURL:[_document fileURL] forSaveOperation:UIDocumentSaveForOverwriting
completionHandler:^(BOOL success) {
        [_document closeWithCompletionHandler:^(BOOL success) {
            dispatch_async(dispatch_get_main_queue(), ^{
                if(!success){
                    NSLog(@"Failed to close - %@",[_document fileURL]);
                }
```

```
            [_delegate detailViewControllerDidClose:self];
        });
    }];
  }];
}
```

Here we call the saveToURL:forSaveOperation:completionHandler: method to save the document. Inside our completion handler we call the closeWithCompletionHandler: method to close the document. And finally inside of its completion handle we use a dispatch_async call against the main thread to call our delegate method detailViewControllerDidClose and pass ourselves as the parameter.

The final three things we need to do are back in the FriendsCollectionViewController.m file so open it back up. Let's move to our detailViewControllerDidClose method and adjust it to look like this.

```
-(void)detailViewControllerDidClose:(FriendDetailViewController *)detailViewController {
    [self.navigationController popToRootViewControllerAnimated:YES];

    NSFileVersion *version = [NSFileVersion currentVersionOfItemAtURL:[detailViewController.document
fileURL]];
    [self addOrUpdateEntryWithURL:[detailViewController.document fileURL]
metadata:[detailViewController.document metadata] state:[detailViewController.document
documentState] version:version];
}
```

We are making the same call to popToRootViewControllerAnimated as we did previously. But now we pull the file version of the document using the NSFileVersion method currentVersionOfItemAtURL:. Then we call our method addOrUpdateEntryWithURL:metadata:state:version with all the documents details.

Next we need to update our alert message in entryCollectionViewCell:longPressedForEntry: to display the display name of the document we want to delete. The line where we instantiate the UIAlertView should now look like this:

```
UIAlertView *alert = [[UIAlertView alloc] initWithTitle:@"Delete Entry" message:[NSString
stringWithFormat:@"Are you sure you want to delete the entry for %@",[[entry metadata] displayName]]
delegate:self cancelButtonTitle:@"No" otherButtonTitles:@"Yes",nil];
```

Lastly we need to update our prepareForSegue: method so that we pass the selectedDocument to the FriendDetailViewController. It should now look like this:

```
#pragma mark - Navigation
- (void)prepareForSegue:(UIStoryboardSegue *)segue sender:(id)sender
{
    if([segue.identifier isEqualToString:@"ToFriendDetails"]){
        [[segue destinationViewController] setDelegate:self];
        [[segue destinationViewController] setDocument:_selectedDocument];
        [[segue destinationViewController] setShouldStartEditing:_shouldStartEditing];
    }
}
```

You can now build and run your app. You should be able to save, edit, and delete documents. Next we will add iCloud integration so that you can persist this data across all your devices.

Implementing CTDocument with iCloud

The first thing we want to do is check and see whether iCloud is even available on the phone. In order to do that we call a method on NSFileManager called URLForUbiquityContainer:. This method returns nil if iCloud is not available, but if it is available it gives us the NSURL for the iCloud/ Ubiquity container. Let's start off by creating two public properties in our CTAppDelegate.h file.

```
@property (strong) NSURL *iCloudURL;
@property BOOL iCloudIsAvailable;
```

Next we will move to our CTAppDelegate.m file and create a method that will take a block as its parameter.

```
-(void)initializeiCloudAccessWithCompletionHandler:(void(^)(BOOL isAvailable)) completion {
    dispatch_async(dispatch_get_global_queue(DISPATCH_QUEUE_PRIORITY_DEFAULT, 0), ^{
        _iCloudURL = [[NSFileManager defaultManager] URLForUbiquityContainerIdentifier:nil];
        if(_iCloudURL != nil){
            dispatch_async(dispatch_get_main_queue(), ^{
                NSLog(@"iCloud is available - %@",_iCloudURL);
                completion(TRUE);
            });
        } else {
            dispatch_async(dispatch_get_main_queue(), ^{
                NSLog(@"iCloud is not available");
                completion(FALSE);
            });
        }
    });
}
```

We start by creating a dispatch_async block to run this on a background thread. The reason we do this is that the method URLForUbiquityContainerIdentifier: may respond immediately or it could even take a few seconds. Because this is an unknown and we don't want to block the UI thread, we run this on a background thread. We assign the result of URLForUbiquityContainerIdentifier: to our public property _iCloudURL.

Next we check to see if it is not nil. If it isn't, we move back to the main thread and call our completion block passing it a value of TRUE. If it is nil, then we move back to the main thread and call our completion block passing it a value of FALSE.

Now we need to call this method, but when should we call it? We want to call this method whenever the application becomes active. Because the user could move from the app to turn iCloud on or off we want to check our iCloud status as soon as the app is active again. Because of that, we will put the method call in the applicationDidBecomeActive: method.

```
- (void)applicationDidBecomeActive:(UIApplication *)application
{
    [self initializeiCloudAccessWithCompletionHandler:^(BOOL isAvailable) {
        _iCloudIsAvailable = isAvailable;
    }];
}
```

Here we call the method we just created. In the block we just take the isAvailable BOOL value and assign it to our public property _iCloudIsAvailable.

Controlling iCloud with Settings

We need to give the user the ability to turn iCloud on or off. This is best handled in Settings for the app because it will remain out of the way of our content, but will give the user a place to go if they want to turn it on or off. Adding this is an easy process. We start by adding a new file that is a Settings Bundle. This can be found under the iOS ➤ Resource category when adding a new file as shown in Figure 5-1. The name by default is Settings, which is fine for what we need.

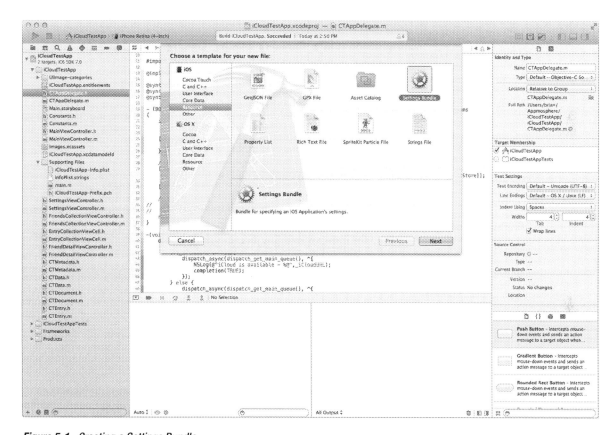

Figure 5-1. Creating a Settings Bundle

If you expand the Settings.bundle in your Project Navigator you should see a file named Root.plist. Select that file so we can look at it.

This plist has a root node that is a dictionary. It is called "iPhone Settings Schema." Inside there is an array named "Preference Items." And inside that you should have four Dictionaries. To keep things simple we want to delete all of them except the item that has a toggle switch.

Now expand the item that is the toggle switch and let's change a few things. We want our default value to be set to "NO." The reason behind this is that you don't want to force anyone to use iCloud. Think of this as an added feature for your user. Next we want to change the Identifier to "ICLOUD_ON." Now change the title to "Use iCloud."

That's all we need to do to add our app to Settings and give the user a setting that they can change. You can build and run your app to see it in action. But we aren't using it just yet. We will get to that soon.

A Few More Constants

Let's set the table now by adding a few more constants to our constants class files. In the .h file add the following declarations.

```
NSString * const CTiCloudOn;
NSString * const CTiCloudWasOn;
NSString * const CTPromptedForiCloud;
Now, lets assign these a value in the .m file.
NSString * const CTiCloudOn = @"ICLOUD_ON";
NSString * const CTiCloudWasOn = @"ICLOUD_WAS_ON";
NSString * const CTPromptedForiCloud = @"PROMPTED_FOR_ICLOUD";
```

Many Different States

When integrating iCloud we need to determine the possible states in which our app could be used. Is the user on iCloud or are they not on iCloud? Have they been on iCloud?

There are four states that we are going to concern ourselves with. They are

- iCloud has been turned on for the first time.

- iCloud has been switched off.

- iCloud isn't available, but it was previously on.

- iCloud isn't on, but it is available.

To help us determine the state, we add a few helper methods inside of our FriendsCollectionViewController.m file.

```
#pragma mark - Helpers
-(BOOL)iCloudOn {
    return [[NSUserDefaults standardUserDefaults] boolForKey:CTiCloudOn];
}

-(void)setiCloudOn:(BOOL)on {
    [[NSUserDefaults standardUserDefaults] setBool:on forKey:CTiCloudOn];
    [[NSUserDefaults standardUserDefaults] synchronize];
}

-(BOOL)iCloudWasOn {
    return [[NSUserDefaults standardUserDefaults] boolForKey:CTiCloudWasOn];
}
```

```
-(void)setiCloudWasOn:(BOOL)on {
    [[NSUserDefaults standardUserDefaults] setBool:on forKey:CTiCloudWasOn];
    [[NSUserDefaults standardUserDefaults] synchronize];
}

-(BOOL)promptedForiCloud {
    return [[NSUserDefaults standardUserDefaults] boolForKey:CTPromptedForiCloud];
}

-(void)setPromptedForiCloud:(BOOL)prompted {
    [[NSUserDefaults standardUserDefaults] setBool:prompted forKey:CTPromptedForiCloud];
    [[NSUserDefaults standardUserDefaults] synchronize];
}
```

We have getters and setters to determine if iCloud is on or was on and we also have one for our
iCloud prompt. We want to make sure that we aren't prompting the user continuously if they have
already said they don't want to use iCloud. Now let's modify our reload method so that we handle
these different states.

```
-(void)reload {
    [_entries removeAllObjects];
    [self.collectionView reloadData];

    [self.navigationItem.rightBarButtonItem setEnabled:NO];

    if([AppDelegate iCloudIsAvailable]){
        if(![self iCloudOn] && ![self promptedForiCloud]){
            [self setPromptedForiCloud:YES];

            UIAlertView *alert = [[UIAlertView alloc] initWithTitle:@"iCloud is available"
message:@"Would you like to store you documents in the cloud to keep them up-to-date across all of
your devices?" delegate:self cancelButtonTitle:@"Not Now" otherButtonTitles:@"Yes", nil];
            [alert setTag:2];
            [alert show];
        }

        //Move files if newly switched on or off
        if([self iCloudOn] && ![self iCloudWasOn]){
        //TODO #1 move data to iCloud
        } else if(![self iCloudOn] && [self iCloudWasOn]){
            //TODO #2 copy data from iCloud
        }

        //TODO #3 get iCloud files

        [self setiCloudWasOn:[self iCloudOn]];
    } else {
        [self setPromptedForiCloud:NO];
```

```
    if([self iCloudWasOn]){
        [[[UIAlertView alloc] initWithTitle:@"iCloud Not Available" message:@"You are currently
unable to connect to iCloud so updates to your documents will not take place until you are connected
to iCloud again." delegate:nil cancelButtonTitle:@"OK" otherButtonTitles:nil] show];
    }

    [self setiCloudOn:NO];
    [self setiCloudWasOn:NO];
    }

    if(![self iCloudOn])
        [self loadLocal];
}
```

The first two lines of this method are identical to what we had before. Next we disable the add button because we don't want the user to have the ability to add while we are pulling our data.

In the next line we check to see whether iCloud is available. If iCloud is available, we then check to see if it is not on and we have not prompted the user. If we pass that test, then we start by calling our setPromptForiCloud: method with a value of YES. We follow this by creating an alert view that will prompt the user to determine whether they want to use iCloud. We set the tag to our alert to 2 so that we can handle it correctly in our alertView:clickedButtonAtIndex: method.

We then check to see if iCloud is on and if iCloud was not on previously, which lets us know that the user just turned iCloud on for the first time. If that state is true, we have a TODO item that we will write later that will move the local data to the iCloud container. We follow that with an else if to check whether iCloud is not on and iCloud was on previously signaling that the user has just turned iCloud off. If this state is true, we have a TODO item that we will write later that will handle copying data from the iCloud container to our local directory. We follow up all this by calling our setiCloudWasOn: method with the current value return from iCloudOn.

If the iCloud is not available, we first call our method setPromptedForiCloud: and passing NO. We do this because we want to make sure that if the user hasn't had a chance to turn iCloud on they will be prompted once iCloud is available.

Next we check to see if iCloudWasOn so that we can alert the user and let them know that iCloud is currently not available. We set the delegate to nil on this alertView because we are just notifying the user and not expecting any decision to made by them. We then call setiCloudOn and setiCloudWasOn to NO because it isn't available. Setting these values is what allows the user to work locally, but then when iCloud connectivity is regained any local data will be pushed to iCloud.

In the last piece of code we check to see whether iCloud is on. If it isn't, then we call our loadLocal method to load our local data. Now let's move on to our alertView delegate method and handle the alertView whose tag we set to 2. We will add an else if statement like this:

```
} else if(alertView.tag == 2){
    if(buttonIndex == alertView.firstOtherButtonIndex){
        [self setiCloudOn:YES];
        [self reload];
    }
}
```

Because we are handling the loading of our data in our reload method we only need to check to see if the user selected "Yes" to use iCloud. If they did, we call setiCloudOn: and pass YES. Then we call our reload method again.

Now we need to start adding some iCloud specific methods. At the bottom of the file, right above the @end line, let's add a pragma mark and start adding methods.

The first method we will add will create an NSMetadataQuery object. An NSMetadataQuery is a query that is specific to iCloud. It allows us to write a query that will first give us results, but it will also continue to check for changes without calling it again and again. We could write this creation of this query inline, but abstracting it out to its own method will allow for better readability of our overall code. Let's write this method now.

```
-(NSMetadataQuery *)documentQuery {
    NSMetadataQuery *query = [[NSMetadataQuery alloc] init];
    if(query){
        [query setSearchScopes:@[NSMetadataQueryUbiquitousDocumentsScope]];

        NSPredicate *predicate = [NSPredicate predicateWithFormat:@"%K LIKE %@",NSMetadataItemFSName
Key,[NSString stringWithFormat:@"*.%@",CT_EXTENSION]];
        [query setPredicate:predicate];
    }

    return query;
}
```

First alloc and init an NSMetadataQuery object. We then check to be sure our object was created successfully. Next we call the setSearchScopes: method on our query object and pass it an array that consists of one value, nSMetadataQueryUbiquitiousDocumentsScope. Here we are telling our query that we only want to search for files in the Documents directory of the application iCloud container directories. We then write a predicate to confine our search even more. Our predicate says we want all File System file names that are LIKE *.ict. We apply this newly created predicate by calling setPredicate on our NSMetadataQuery object. Finally we return our query object.

Now we need to write two more methods. One will start our query and another will stop it.

```
-(void)queryiCloud {
    [self stopiCloudQuery];
    _query = [self documentQuery];

    [[NSNotificationCenter defaultCenter] addObserver:self selector:@selector(processiCloudFiles:)
name:NSMetadataQueryDidFinishGatheringNotification object:nil];
    [[NSNotificationCenter defaultCenter] addObserver:self selector:@selector(processiCloudFiles:)
name:NSMetadataQueryDidUpdateNotification object:nil];
    [_query startQuery];
}

-(void)stopiCloudQuery {
    if(_query){
        [[NSNotificationCenter defaultCenter] removeObserver:self
name:NSMetadataQueryDidFinishGatheringNotification object:nil];
```

```
        [[NSNotificationCenter defaultCenter] removeObserver:self
name:NSMetadataQueryDidUpdateNotification object:nil];
        [_query stopQuery];
        _query = nil;
    }
}
```

The queryiCloud method starts out by calling our stopiCloudQuery method which does exactly that. We will go into more detail on how it does that shortly. Then we call our documentQuery method that we just created and assign the return value to our private _query property. But, we haven't created that so let's do that now. In the private interface add this line:

```
@property (strong) NSMetadataQuery *query;
```

Now that we have our query property created and assigned let's move on. In the next two lines we add our self as an observer for two messages that will be fired by our NSMetadataQuery. They are NSMetadataQueryDidDidFinishGatheringNotification and NSMetadataQueryDidUpdateNotification. We tell notification center that when these messages or notifications are fired we want to call our processiCloudFiles: method. We will write that shortly. We end our method call by calling the startQuery method on our NSMetadataQuery object.

Our stopiCloudQuery method is similar. We first check to see if query is not nil. If it is, then we remove ourselves as the observer for both of the messages we subscribed to earlier. Then we call stopQuery on our NSMetadataQuey object and finally set our object to nil.

Before we can write our processiCloudFiles: method we need to add a few more private properties. In the private interface add the following:

```
@property (strong) NSMutableArray *iCloudURLs;
@property BOOL iCloudIsReady;
@property BOOL awaitingMoveLocalToiCloud;
@property BOOL awaitingCopyiCloudToLocal;
```

Let's also not forget to initialize the iCloudURLs array. In your viewDidLoad: add an initialization for iCloudURLs just above the line where you initialize your entries array.

```
_iCloudURLs = [NSMutableArray array];
```

Now we can write our processiCloudFiles: method.

```
-(void)processiCloudFiles:(NSNotification *)notification {
    [_query disableUpdates];

    [_iCloudURLs removeAllObjects];

    [[_query results] enumerateObjectsUsingBlock:^(NSMetadataItem *item,
NSUInteger idx, BOOL *stop) {
        NSURL *fileURL = [item valueForAttribute:NSMetadataItemURLKey];
        NSNumber *aBool = nil;
```

```
        [fileURL getResourceValue:&aBool forKey:NSURLIsHiddenKey error:nil];
        if(aBool && ![aBool boolValue]){
            [_iCloudURLs addObject:fileURL];
        }
    }];

    NSLog(@"Found %i files in iCloud",[_iCloudURLs count]);
    _iCloudIsReady = YES;

    if([self iCloudOn]){
        for(NSInteger i = [_entries count] - 1; i >= 0; i--){
            CTEntry *entry = _entries[i];
            if(![_iCloudURLs containsObject:[entry fileURL]]){
                [self removeEntryWithURL:[entry fileURL]];
            }
        }

        [_iCloudURLs enumerateObjectsUsingBlock:^(NSURL *fileURL, NSUInteger idx, BOOL *stop) {
            [self loadDocumentAtFileURL:fileURL];
        }];

        [self.navigationItem.rightBarButtonItem setEnabled:YES];
    }

    [_query enableUpdates];

    if(_awaitingMoveLocalToiCloud) {
        _awaitingMoveLocalToiCloud = NO;

        //TODO #1 move data to iCloud

    } else if(_awaitingCopyiCloudToLocal){

        //TODO #2 copy data from iCloud
    }
}
```

We start off by calling disableUpdates on our NSMetadataQuery object. We do this because our result set could change. Calling disableUpdates makes sure that the data set we are going to enumerate over is not going to change on us. We follow this up by clearing our iCloudURLs array because we will be enumerating over all files and not just new ones.

Next we use the enumerateObjectsUsingBlock: method on the results array inside our NSMetadataQuery object. It holds an array of NSMetadataItems. Inside this block we start by getting the NSURL for the file by calling valueForAttribute and passing it the NSMetadataItemURLKey key. We then create an NSNumber object called aBool and set it to nil.

Next we check to see if this is a hidden file by calling the method getResourceValue:forKey:error method on the NSURL object fileURL. We pass the pointer of our NSNumber aBool and the key NSURLIsHiddenKey. Then we check to see if aBool is not nil and if it is set to NO which means the file is not a hidden file. If this statement is true we add the fileURL object to our iCloudURLs array.

We then set our iCloudIsReady property to YES. This value is going to be used in the methods we will write to move data to iCloud or to copy data from iCloud.

Next we check to see if iCloudOn returns true. If it is, then we first want to clean up our entries array by checking if any of our entry fileURLS match an object in our iCloudURLs. If it does, we remove that entry by calling removeEntryWithURL: and pass the fileURL. This is done to make sure we don't end up with duplicate entries because next we will enumerate over our iCloudURLs array and call loadDocumentAtFileURL: and pass the fileURL. If you follow this method you will see that a CTEntry object will get created and added to our entries array. The last step is to re enable our add button. If you recall we disabled this when we first called our reload method.

We then want to enable updates by calling the enableUpdates method on our NSMetadataQuery object. The final thing we do here is check to see if we are awaiting a move of our local data to iCloud or if we are awaiting copying our iCloud document to our local directory. If we are wanting to move our local data to iCloud we set our bool to NO. Each of our TODOs will be the actual method calls that we will write now.

The first method is going to copy our local files to iCloud and should look like this:

```
-(void)moveLocalToiCloud {
    if(_iCloudIsReady && !_awaitingMoveLocalToiCloud){
        NSArray *localDocuments = [[NSFileManager defaultManager]
contentsOfDirectoryAtURL:[AppDelegate applicationDocumentsDirectory] includingPropertiesForKeys:nil
options:0 error:nil];
        [localDocuments enumerateObjectsUsingBlock:^(NSURL *fileURL, NSUInteger idx, BOOL *stop) {
            if([[fileURL pathExtension] isEqualToString:CT_EXTENSION]){
                NSString *fileName = [[fileURL lastPathComponent] stringByDeletingPathExtension];
                NSURL *destinationURL = [self getDocumentURL:[self getDocumentFilename:fileName
forLocal:NO]];

                dispatch_async(dispatch_get_global_queue(DISPATCH_QUEUE_PRIORITY_DEFAULT, 0), ^{
                    NSError *error = nil;
                    BOOL success = [[NSFileManager defaultManager] setUbiquitous:[self iCloudOn]
itemAtURL:fileURL destinationURL:destinationURL error:&error];
                    if(success){
                        NSLog(@"Moved %@ to %@",fileURL,destinationURL);
                        [self loadDocumentAtFileURL:destinationURL];
                    } else {
                        NSLog(@"Error Moving %@ to %@ - %@",fileURL,destinationURL,error.
localizedDescription);
                    }
                });
            }
        }];
    } else {
        _awaitingMoveLocalToiCloud = YES;
    }
}
```

We start this method of by checking to see whether iCloudIsReady and to be sure we are awaiting a move of our local data to iCloud. This may seem a little strange because we are in this method, but we are making sure that iCloud is ready. If we are truly ready to move our local data to iCloud, we move on. If not, we set out _awaitingMoveLocalToiCloud back to YES.

We start by getting an array of NSURLs for the documents that reside in our applications documents directory. Next we enumerate that array. For each NSURL in that array we check to be sure the path extension matches our ict document extension. If it does get the destination URL by calling getDocumentURL: and passing it the value returned from getDocumentFiles:forLocal:. then we pass our filename without the extension and the final parameter of NO. We will modify that method shortly to handle iCloud. But it is safe to assume at this point that we get back an iCloud URL.

Now we move to a background thread by calling dispatch_async. Using NSFileManager we call the method setUbiquitous:itemAtURL:destinationURL:error:, which will move our file from the local directory and put it in the iCloud container. We check to see whether we were successful and if so we call loadDocumentAtFileURL: passing it our destinationURL. Remember that this method will end up creating our CTEntry object or updating it if necessary. If we weren't successful, we log out the error so you can see what might have happened. Now let's write the method to copy our documents from iCloud to our local directory.

```
-(void)copyiCloudToLocal {
    if(_iCloudIsReady && _awaitingCopyiCloudToLocal){
        _awaitingCopyiCloudToLocal = NO;

        [_iCloudURLs enumerateObjectsUsingBlock:^(NSURL *fileURL, NSUInteger idx, BOOL *stop) {
            NSString *fileName = [[fileURL lastPathComponent] stringByDeletingPathExtension];
            NSURL *destinationURL = [self getDocumentURL:[self getDocumentFilename:fileName
forLocal:YES]];

            dispatch_async(dispatch_get_global_queue(DISPATCH_QUEUE_PRIORITY_DEFAULT, 0), ^{
                NSFileCoordinator *fileCoordinator = [[NSFileCoordinator alloc]
initWithFilePresenter:nil];
                [fileCoordinator coordinateReadingItemAtURL:fileURL
options:NSFileCoordinatorReadingWithoutChanges error:nil byAccessor:^(NSURL *newURL) {
                    NSFileManager *fileManager = [[NSFileManager alloc] init];
                    NSError *error = nil;

                    BOOL success = [fileManager copyItemAtURL:fileURL toURL:destinationURL
error:&error];
                    if(success){
                        NSLog(@"Copied %@ to %@",fileURL,destinationURL);
                        [self loadDocumentAtFileURL:destinationURL];
                    } else {
                        NSLog(@"Error Copying %@ to %@ - %@",fileURL,destinationURL,
error.localizedDescription);
                    }
                }];
            });
        }];
```

```
    } else {
        if(!_awaitingCopyiCloudToLocal){
            UIAlertView *alert = [[UIAlertView alloc] initWithTitle:@"Turning iCloud Off"
message:@"What would you like to do with the documents currently on iCloud?" delegate:self
cancelButtonTitle:@"Keep Using iCloud" otherButtonTitles:@"Keep a local copy",@"Keep only on
iCloud", nil];
            [alert setTag:3];
            [alert show];
        }
    }
}
```

The start of this method is very similar to the previous one. We first check to see if we are awaitingCopyiCloudToLocal and iCloudIsReady. If it is, then we start the copy process, however if it isn't, we check to see whether _awaitingCopyiCloudToLocal is set to NO. If it is, then we create an alertView and ask the user if they would like to keep using iCloud, Keep a local copy, or Keep a copy only on iCloud. We set the tag of this alert to 3 so we can handle it correctly and then call show.

If we are going to copy the iCloud files to our local directory, we first set our _awaitingCopyiCloudToLocal BOOL value to NO. Then we enumerate through our iCloudURLs array. We then use the same method we used in the previous method to get our destinationURL except this time we pass YES for the last parameter.

We then create a block that will run on the background thread by calling dispatch_async. We create an NSFileCoordinator and call the method coordinateReadingItemAtURL:op tions:error:byAccessor: method. We pass in the iCloud URL and pass it an option of NSFileCoordinatorReadingWithoutChanges. In our byAccessor: block we create an NSFileManager object and then call copyItemAtURL:toURL:error:. Finally, we call the loadDocumentAtFileURL method passing our destinationURL.

Now let's go modify our alertView to handle this new alert dialog.

```
} else if(alertView.tag == 3){
    if(buttonIndex == alertView.cancelButtonIndex){
        [self setiCloudOn:YES];
        [self reload];
    } else if(buttonIndex == alertView.firstOtherButtonIndex){
        _awaitingCopyiCloudToLocal = YES;
        if(_iCloudIsReady){
            [self copyiCloudToLocal];
        }
    }
}
```

Here we check to see if the user selected "Keep using iCloud." If they did, we set iCloudOn and then call reload. Next we see if they selected "Keep a local copy." If they did we set our _awaitingCopyiCloudToLocal to YES. If iCloud is ready then we call copyiCloudToLocal. The final selection "Keep only on iCloud" is an action we don't need to worry about because there data is already on iCloud.

Now, let's go to the two spots that we have TODO #1 and change them to read:

```
[self moveLocalToiCloud];
```

And change our TODO #2s to read:

```
[self copyiCloudToLocal];
```

And let's change our TODO #3 to read:

```
[self queryiCloud];
```

Finally let's add the following two lines at the beginning of our reload method.

```
_iCloudIsReady = NO;
    [_iCloudURLs removeAllObjects];
```

Now we need to modify our getDocumentFilename:forLocal method so that we are handling a value of NO for the last parameter. Currently we only check to see whether the value isLocal is YES. We need to add an else to that statement so we can check to see whether the name exists in our iCloud container. The if statement should now look like this:

```
if(isLocal){
    nameExists = [self documentNameExistsInObjects:newDocName];
} else {
    nameExists = [self documentNameExistsIniCloudURLs:newDocName];
}
```

We are calling a new method here documentNameExistsIniCloudURLs:. Let's write that now.

```
-(BOOL)documentNameExistsIniCloudURLs:(NSString *)documentName {
    __block BOOL nameExists = NO;
    [_iCloudURLs enumerateObjectsUsingBlock:^(NSURL *fileURL, NSUInteger idx, BOOL *stop) {
        if([[fileURL lastPathComponent] isEqualToString:documentName]){
            nameExists = YES;
            *stop = YES;
        }
    }];

    return nameExists;
}
```

This is an identical method to documentNameExistsInObjects: except here we are enumerating through the iCloudURLs array.

The last thing we want to do is to add our self as an observer to the UIApplicationDidBecomeActiveNotification. We do this in the viewWillAppear: method. We add an enableUpdates call on our NSMetadataQuery object as well.

```
-(void)viewWillAppear:(BOOL)animated {
    [super viewWillAppear:animated];

    [[NSNotificationCenter defaultCenter] addObserver:self selector:@selector(didBecomeActive:)
name:UIApplicationDidBecomeActiveNotification object:nil];
    [_query enableUpdates];
}
```

When we add ourselves as the observer we are telling NSNotificationCenter that we want to call our method didBecomeActive:. Let's write that now.

```
-(void)didBecomeActive:(NSNotification *)notification {
    [self reload];
}
```

Here we just call reload when our application becomes active with this screen visible. Now we need to remove ourselves as the observer and disableUpdates on our NSMetadataQuery object in the viewDidDisappear: method.

```
-(void)viewDidDisappear:(BOOL)animated {
    [_query disableUpdates];
    [[NSNotificationCenter defaultCenter] removeObserver:self];
}
```

You may be wondering why we call enableUpdates and disableUpdates in viewWillAppear: and viewDidDisappear:, respectively. We do this to stop our query from firing updates if our view is not visible. This conserves system resources and is responsible programming on our part.

We are done with our programming portion, but we do need to configure our app to handle our ict file extension by defining a document type and a UTI.

1. To do this we need to select our project in the Project Navigator, then select the Info tab in the main window. You will see a section for Document Types. Expand that section and add a new document type by clicking the + button.

2. Set the Name to "iCloudTest Document". Set types to the bundle identifier you created earlier and append a .doc to it. For example mine is com. appmosphereinc.icloudtest.doc.

3. Now expand the additional document type properties by clicking the caret. Click in the box to add a property.

4. The first property we add is of type Boolean and is called "LSTypeIsPackage." Set it to YES.

5. Next, add an array and label it "CFBundleTypeExtensions." Expand the array by clicking the caret and then click the + to add an item in the array. The item should be a string with a value of "ict."

6. The final key we need to add is "LSHandlerRank," which will be a string. Give it a value of "Owner."

7. Now we need to add an Exported UTI. UTI stands for Uniform Type Identifiers. Expand Exported UTIs and click the + button as shown in Figure 5-2.

Figure 5-2. *Creating an exported UTI*

8. As shown in Figure 5-3, we will set the identifier to the same value we used for our document type. In this case it is com.appmosphereinc.icloudtest.doc. We want to set the Confirms To field to com.apple.package. All the other fields can be left blank.

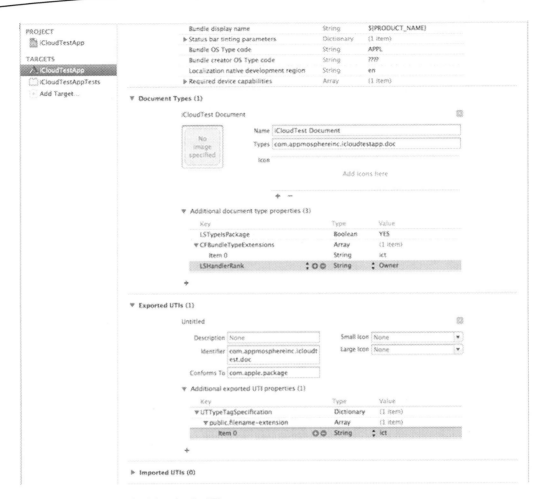

Figure 5-3. Completing the required data for the UTI

9.   Now we need to add an additional exported UTI property by clicking the caret.
     We will add a dictionary and will name it "UTTypeTagSpecification." Expand
     the dictionary and add an array with the name "public.filename-extension."
     Add one string item to the array and give it a value of "ict."

We are done. If you run your project now on a device, you will be prompted to use iCloud. If you
select Yes, then your local data will be copied to iCloud. Then you can remove your application
completely and test to verify that all your data is being persisted on new devices and new installs.
Make changes on one device and watch them appear on the other. The magic of iCloud is at your
fingertips.

Summary

You have now learned how to use UIDocument both locally and with iCloud. Thanks to the enhancements Apple has made to UIDocument this process is fairly simple and straightforward. Moving forward into Chapter 6 we will dip our toes into Core Data, creating a very basic addition to our current app. And as we did with UIDocument, I will walk you through taking Core Data from a local data store and move it up to iCloud. After that we will revisit all these technologies and show you the different methods you can use to test your implementations of iCloud.

Chapter 6

iCloud with Core Data

In this chapter you will learn the fundamentals of integrating iCloud with Core Data. I start by explaining what Core Data is and then move on to the new features recently added to Core Data and iCloud. Next, we will add another section to our app, which utilizes Core Data as its data store. Finally, we will integrate this new section to iCloud.

What Is Core Data?

Core Data, at its base, is an API developed by Apple to handle interaction with a local data store. The Core Data framework provides numerous features. Here are a few:

- Change tracking and undo support
- Relationship maintenance
- Automatic validation of property values
- Schema migration
- Full, automatic support for key-value coding and key-value observing
- Grouping, filtering, and organizing data in memory and in the user interface

There are so many more important features than can be named here. To learn more you can visit the Developer Center at http://developer.apple.com. I would also recommend picking up the book, *Pro Core Data for iOS* by Michael Privat and Robert Warner for an in-depth look at Core Data technologies and how and why to use Core Data.

Apple has made great strides to make iCloud integration into Core Data applications easier than ever. The following sections discuss some of those changes.

Fallback Store

The fallback store is a local persistent store available to your app in the event that the iCloud store was unavailable for a period of time. Until recently, you would add this store to the persistent store coordinator. This made your fallback store available to the managed object context so that the user could continue to make changes while the iCloud store was being set up automatically. This worked great, but there was a downside. If your app interfaced with multiple iCloud accounts, over time you would end up managing a lot of different persistent stores. Basically, you would manage one fallback store and one iCloud store for every account.

Apple has since assumed responsibility of the fallback store so that you no longer need to manage this. You now manage one store, and the API delivers the appropriate store to you. This change also means that you must store your persistent store in local storage.

Core Data Logging

Now that the API has taken over management of the fallback store, you will receive new events logged to the console when you are debugging your app. These events will let you know if you are currently using the fallback store or the iCloud store. Here are the two event logs you will now see and which store they pertain to (see Figure 6-1).

```
(IndexPath *)indexPath
```

```
2013-12-12 12:30:29.308 iCloudTestApp[53580:70b] -[PFUbiquitySwitchboardEntryMetadata setUseLocalStorage:](754): CoreData:
Ubiquity:  brian~simDEB097D8-186C-570C-951D-18366A92E562:Store
Using local storage: 1
2013-12-12 12:30:29.323 iCloudTestApp[53580:70b] iCloud is available - file:///Users/brian/Library/Application%20Support/
iPhone%20Simulator/7.0.3/Library/Mobile%20Documents/ED88G235KU~com~appmosphereinc~icloudtestapp/
2013-12-12 12:30:30.481 iCloudTestApp[53580:1303] store changed
2013-12-12 12:30:30.482 iCloudTestApp[53580:1303] -[PFUbiquitySwitchboardEntryMetadata setUseLocalStorage:](754): CoreData:
Ubiquity:  brian~simDEB097D8-186C-570C-951D-18366A92E562:Store
Using local storage: 0
```

Figure 6-1. iCloud Core Data Log

- Using fallback store

  Core Data: Ubiquity: peerID:StoreName - Using local storage: 1

- Using iCloud store

  Core Data: Ubiquity: peerID:StoreName - Using local storage: 0

Asynchronous Setup

In the past, the API handled persistent store setup synchronously. This solution was fine when you were just bringing a local store online, because that process is extremely fast. But in the event that you were using iCloud, this process could take a significant amount of time to ensure the iCloud store was ready for use.

Because the fallback store is now managed by the API, this process is asynchronous. In the event that the iCloud store is not ready for use, the API will return the fallback store for us to use. With this change, Apple has added two notifications that we will interact with. These are

- `NSPersistentStoreCoordinatorStoresWillChangeNotification`: Fired when the store changes to give you a chance to save any changes prior to the change.

- `NSPersistentStoreCoordinatorStoresDidChangeNotification`: Called after the store changed and may be used to update any UI if needed.

It is important to note that these notifications are only fired in the event that the persistent store actually changes. If your user has already launched your app previously using their iCloud account, these notifications will not be fired. The reason for this is that the iCloud persistent store will be immediately available even if there are pending changes that need to be pulled from iCloud. Any changes pulled from iCloud will be notified using `NSPersistentStoreDidImportUbiquitousContentChangesNotification` just as they have previously.

iCloud account changes are handled with the same notifications that you use for asynchronous setup. You no longer need to subscribe to the `NSUbiquityIdentityTokenDidChangeNotification` because the Core Data API will notify you of a store change using the previously mentioned `willChange` and `didChange` notifications.

Now that I have explained the updated features to Core Data using iCloud, let's begin adding another section of our app that will use Core Data.

Closest Friends

Because we are keeping track of our friends, I thought it might be nice to also keep track of our closest friends. Rather than worry about their current age, as we do with our friends, it is more appropriate to keep track of their birthday so we don't accidently miss that important day. In this section we will add a new tab for our closest friends. Selecting that tab will take us to a Table View listing of our closest friends, and we will have a similar detail screen as the one we use for our regular friends.

Adding the CloseFriend Entity

Let's start by adding an entity to our data model:

1. Select the `iCloudTestApp.datamodeld` to open the data model editor.

2. Select the Add Entity button.

3. Change the entity name to `CloseFriend`.

4. Add four attributes
    - ▦ `birthday`
        - ▦ **Type:** Date
    - ▦ `firstName`
        - ▦ **Type:** String
    - ▦ `lastName`
        - ▦ **Type:** String
    - ▦ `image`
        - ▦ **Type:** BinaryData

5. Create a new group under `iCloudTestApp` and name it `ManagedObjects`.

6. With the `ManagedObjects` group selected, create a new `NSManagedObject` subclass. This template is found under Core Data in the iOS section.

7. Make sure `iCloudTestApp` is selected for the data model and click Next.

8. Select `CloseFriend` and click Next.

9. Create a new folder for this file and call is `ManagedObjects`.

10. Make sure the `iCloudTestApp` target is checked and click Create.

Modifying the Storyboard

Now we need to modify the Storyboard (see Figure 6-2):

1. Select the `Main.storyboard` to open the Storyboard editor.

2. Drag in a Table View Controller.

3. With the new Table View Controller selected, embed a navigation controller.

4. Select the Tab Bar Controller.

5. Ctrl-drag from the Tab Bar Controller to the new navigation controller you just created and select View Controllers under Relationship Segue from the pop-up menu.

6. Select the Tab Bar Item from the Navigation Controller and change the title to **Close Friends**.

7. Drag in a View Controller to the right of the new Table View Controller.

8. Select the Table View Controller.

9. Ctrl-drag from the Table View Controller to the View Controller and select Push from the pop-up menu.

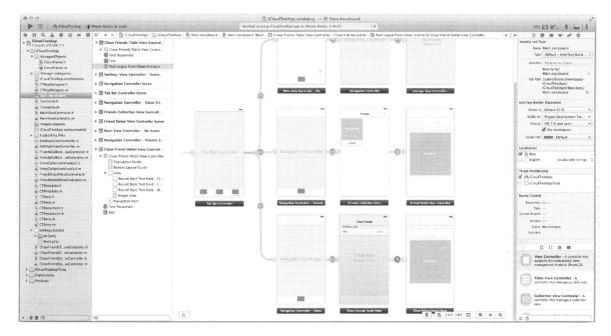

Figure 6-2. Full Storyboard

Configuring the Table View Controller

Next, configure the table view controller:

1. Select the Table View Cell inside the table view.

2. In the Attribute Inspector, change the Identifier to `CloseFriendCell`.

3. Change the style to Right Detail.

4. Change Accessory to Disclosure Indicator.

5. Drag a Bar Button Item to the top right of the navigation bar and change its identifier to Add.

6. Select the Navigation Item and set the title to **Close Friends**.

Configuring the Detail View Controller

Now configure the detail view controller (see Figure 6-3):

1. Select the new UIViewController.

2. Drag three text fields into the view.

3. Set them up as follows:
    - First text field
        - Position & Size: x:20 y:84 width:136 height:30
        - Placeholder Text: First Name
        - Text Alignment: Left
    - Second text field
        - Position & Size: x:164 y:84 width:136 height:30
        - Placeholder Text: Last Name
        - Text Alignment: Left
    - Third text field
        - Position & Size: x:20 y:122 width:280 height:30
        - Placeholder Text: Birthday
        - Text Alignment: Center

4. Now drag a `UIImageView` from the object library and place it at x:20 y:160 width:280 height:280.

5. Under the Attribute Inspector check the User Interaction Enabled box.

6. Lastly, select the segue coming into the view and set its identifier to `ToCloseFriendDetails`.

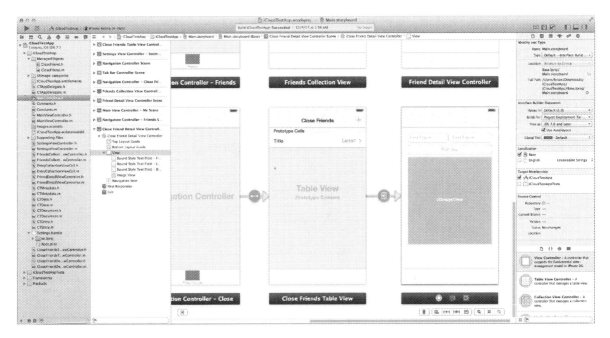

Figure 6-3. Close Friend Detail View Controller

Create View Controller Classes

Now that we have our Storyboard set up, it is time to write the code that will control it. Let's start by creating a new Objective-C class that is a subclass of UITableViewController. Call it CloseFriendsTableViewController.

We need to create another class for our UIViewController that will act as a detail view. Add another Objective-C class that is a subclass of UIViewController and name it CloseFriendDetailViewController.

CloseFriendsTableViewController

Open the CloseFriendsTableViewController.m file and add the import statement for our CloseFriend managed object.

```
#import "CloseFriend.h"
```

Next, let's add some properties to the private interface. These should be self-explanatory.

```
@interface CloseFriendsTableViewController ()
@property (strong) NSArray *closeFriends;
@property (strong) CloseFriend *selectedFriend;
@property BOOL shouldStartEditing;
@end
```

Also, go ahead and delete the initWithStyle: method because we have no use for it. Inside the viewDidLoad: method we need to add a method call to a method named loadCloseFriends. Add the following line just after the [super viewDidLoad]; method call inside the viewDidLoad method.

```
[self loadCloseFriends];
```

Now add the loadCloseFriends method.

```
-(void)loadCloseFriends {
    NSFetchRequest *request = [[NSFetchRequest alloc] init];
    NSEntityDescription *entity = [NSEntityDescription entityForName:@"CloseFriend"
inManagedObjectContext:[AppDelegate managedObjectContext]];
    [request setEntity:entity];

    [request setSortDescriptors:@[[NSSortDescriptor sortDescriptorWithKey:@"lastName"
ascending:YES]]];

    NSError *error = nil;
    NSArray *results = [[AppDelegate managedObjectContext] executeFetchRequest:request
error:&error];
    if(error == nil){
        _closeFriends = results;
    } else {
        NSLog(@"There was an error getting data - %@",error.localizedDescription);
    }
}
```

We start by allocating and initializing an NSFetchRequest object. Then we create our NSEntityDescription by passing the string CloseFriend and our current NSManagedObjectContext to the method entityForName:inManagedObjectContext. Then we set the entity on our request to the entity we just created.

We want our list sorted by last name so we put one NSSortDescriptor in an array and pass that into our request using the method setSortDescriptors:.

The final thing is to execute the fetch request against our managed object context by calling executFetchRequest:error:. Remember that for the error we are passing a pointer to a pointer instead of a pointer to an object. This means that if an error is fired, our error variable is written to directly. This is why in the next line we check to see whether the error is still equal to nil. If it is, we know our fetch request executed properly, so we simply assign our results array to our class property closeFriends. If we did get an error, we use NSLog to print it out so that we can debug it later.

Now we need to add our UITableViewDatasource methods.

```
- (NSInteger)numberOfSectionsInTableView:(UITableView *)tableView
{
    return 1;
}


- (NSInteger)tableView:(UITableView *)tableView numberOfRowsInSection:(NSInteger)section
{
    return [_closeFriends count];
}


- (UITableViewCell *)tableView:(UITableView *)tableView cellForRowAtIndexPath:(NSIndexPath *)
indexPath
{
    static NSString *CellIdentifier = @"CloseFriendCell";
    UITableViewCell *cell = [tableView dequeueReusableCellWithIdentifier:CellIdentifier
forIndexPath:indexPath];

    [self configureCloseFriendCell:cell withFriend:_closeFriends[indexPath.row]];

    return cell;
}


- (BOOL)tableView:(UITableView *)tableView canEditRowAtIndexPath:(NSIndexPath *)indexPath
{
    return YES;
}


- (void)tableView:(UITableView *)tableView commitEditingStyle:(UITableViewCellEditingStyle)
editingStyle forRowAtIndexPath:(NSIndexPath *)indexPath
{
    if (editingStyle == UITableViewCellEditingStyleDelete) {
        [self removeCloseFriend:_closeFriends[indexPath.row]];
        [tableView deleteRowsAtIndexPaths:@[indexPath] withRowAnimation:UITableViewRowAnimationFade];
    }
}
```

This is similar to what we used on the collection view in the previous chapter. We did, however, add two more datasource methods here. The first, tableView:canEditRowAtIndexPath: is used to allow editing, or in our case, deleting. We return YES from this method to turn editing on.

The second method tableView:commitEditingStyle:forRowAtIndexPath: is called when we press the delete button. We check the editing style to make sure we are deleting, and if we are, we call our method removeCloseFriend: and pass the CloseFriend managed object. Next we call a method against our tableView deleteRowsAtIndexPaths:withRowAnimation:. Because we are only deleting one object, we pass an array with the current indexPath. The final parameter we pass is UITableViewRowAnimationFade so that when the cell is removed it is faded out.

We call the method configureCloseFriendCell:withFriend: in the tableView:cellForRowAtIndexPath: method:

```
-(void)configureCloseFriendCell:(UITableViewCell *)cell withFriend:(CloseFriend *)closeFriend {
    static NSDateFormatter *dateFormatter = nil;
    if (dateFormatter == nil) {
        dateFormatter = [[NSDateFormatter alloc] init];
        [dateFormatter setDateStyle:NSDateFormatterShortStyle];
    }

    NSMutableString *name = [NSMutableString stringWithString:@""];
    NSString *birthday = @"";

    if(![[closeFriend firstName] isEqualToString:@""])
        [name appendString:[NSString stringWithFormat:@"%@ ",[closeFriend firstName]]];
    if(![[closeFriend lastName] isEqualToString:@""])
        [name appendString:[closeFriend lastName]];

    if([name isEqualToString:@""])
        [name appendString:@"Undefined"];

    cell.textLabel.text = name;

    if([closeFriend birthday] != nil)
        birthday = [dateFormatter stringFromDate:[closeFriend birthday]];

    cell.detailTextLabel.text = birthday;

    if([closeFriend image] != nil)
        cell.imageView.image = [UIImage imageWithData:[closeFriend image]];
    else
        cell.imageView.image = nil;
}
```

The first thing we do in this method is set a static NSDateFormatter. We do this because we don't want to create a new NSDateFormatter every time we configure a cell. We could use a property for this, but because we are only using the date formatter in this method, a static variable is sufficient.

Next, we create two variables that we will eventually use in our cell labels. We use NSMutableString for the name because we want to use both the first name and last name, or only first name or last name if the other is not present. Finally, if none are present, we set the name variable to the string Undefined.

We then check to see whether the birthday property on our CloseFriend managedObject is set. If it is, we use the static date formatter to get a string representation of the date and assign it to our birthday variable. Then we assign our birthday variable to the cell's detailTextLabel text property.

Finally, we check to see whether our CloseFriend object has an image. If it does, we convert the NSData that we do have stored in the object to a UIImage by calling the imageWithData: class method for UIImage. If we don't have an image, we set the image to nil. Setting the cell's image property is not required, but it is a secondary means for us to make sure that there is no image set when a cell is dequeued.

We still need to write our removeCloseFriend: method so we can add that now.

```
-(void)removeCloseFriend:(CloseFriend *)closeFriend {
    NSMutableArray *closeFriends = _closeFriends.mutableCopy;
    [closeFriends removeObject:closeFriend];

    _closeFriends = closeFriends;

    [[AppDelegate managedObjectContext] deleteObject:closeFriend];
    NSError *error = nil;
    if(![[AppDelegate managedObjectContext] save:&error]){
        NSLog(@"There was an error deleting data - %@",error.localizedDescription);
    }
}
```

We start by creating a mutable copy of our closeFriends class property so we can modify it. Then we remove the closeFriend object that we passed into this method. Then we assign our local closeFriends mutable array to our closeFriends class property so that we now have an NSArray with the object removed that we wanted to remove. The last bit is Core Data specific. We first call deleteObject: against our manageObjectContext and pass it the object we want to delete. Then we call the save: method on our managedObjectContext to save this change. This method returns a BOOL, so we just check to see if it was not successful. If it wasn't, we log our error for later debugging.

Now we need to add our Table View Delegate Methods. In our case we will only be adding one, but there are quite a number of them at your disposal should you have a need for any of them.

```
#pragma mark - UITableViewDelegate Methods
-(void)tableView:(UITableView *)tableView didSelectRowAtIndexPath:(NSIndexPath *)indexPath {
    _selectedFriend = _closeFriends[indexPath.row];
    _shouldStartEditing = NO;
    [self performSegueWithIdentifier:@"ToCloseFriendDetails" sender:nil];
}
```

In this method we simply set the property selectedFriend by getting the object at the index passed to us. We set shouldStartEditing to NO, similar to what we did in the Collection View. Then we call our segue by calling the performSegueWithIdentifier:sender: method and pass ToCloseFriendDetails as the identifier.

Now we need to add the IBAction that will be called when the user presses the add button:

```
#pragma mark - Button Methods
-(IBAction)btnAddPressed:(id)sender {
    CloseFriend *closeFriend = [NSEntityDescription insertNewObjectForEntityForName:@"CloseFriend"
inManagedObjectContext:[AppDelegate managedObjectContext]];
    _selectedFriend = closeFriend;
    _shouldStartEditing = YES;

    [self loadCloseFriends];
    [self performSegueWithIdentifier:@"ToCloseFriendDetails" sender:nil];
}
```

This starts off with another Core Data method. We create our CloseFriend managed object by calling a class method on NSEntityDescription with the signature insertNewObjectForEntityForName: inManagedObjectContext:. We use our object name as the first parameter and pass our managed object context as the second. Then we set our selectedFriend property and our shouldStartEditing property. We set editing to YES in this case because we have a blank object. Finally we call our loadCloseFriends method to reload our closeFriends array and then call our segue. Let's write our prepareForSegue:sender: method now.

```
#pragma mark - Navigation
- (void)prepareForSegue:(UIStoryboardSegue *)segue sender:(id)sender
{
    if([segue.identifier isEqualToString:@"ToCloseFriendDetails"]){
        [[segue destinationViewController] setDelegate:self];
        [[segue destinationViewController] setCloseFriend:_selectedFriend];
        [[segue destinationViewController] setShouldStartEditing:_shouldStartEditing];
    }
}
```

Here we are just assigning our self as the delegate for the CloseFriendDetailViewController, sending our property _selectedFriend and sending our property _shouldStartEditing. Remember, _shouldStartEditing is the Boolean value that determines if we launch the view in edit mode, or if we are just viewing.

CloseFriendDetailViewController

Now we can lay the foundation for the CloseFriendDetailViewController. Select the CloseFriend DetailViewController.h file and let's get to work. We start by adding an import statement for our CloseFriend managed object just above the UIKit import.

```
#import "CloseFriend.h"
```

Next we define the protocol for our `CloseFriendDetailViewControllerDelegate`. Add this line just above the `@interface` line.

```
@protocol CloseFriendDetailViewControllerDelegate;
```

Next, we subscribe to four delegate protocols that we use in the implementation file. They are `UITextFieldDelegate`, `UINavigationControllerDelegate`, `UIActionSheetDelegate`, and `UIImagePickerControllerDelegate`. One thing to note here is that we aren't actually calling any methods on the `UINavigationControllerDelegate`, but the `UIImagePickerControllerDelegate` does require that we subscribe to it because it will be using methods on our behalf.

```
@interface CloseFriendDetailViewController : UIViewController <UITextFieldDelegate,
UINavigationControllerDelegate, UIActionSheetDelegate, UIImagePickerControllerDelegate>
```

Next we define some public properties inside the interface:

```
@property (strong, nonatomic) CloseFriend *closeFriend;
@property (assign) id<CloseFriendDetailViewControllerDelegate> delegate;
@property BOOL shouldStartEditing;
```

The last thing we need to do is define our actual delegate protocol. We add a delegate method `detailViewControllerDidClose:` and we pass this controller as its parameter.

```
@protocol CloseFriendDetailViewControllerDelegate <NSObject>
-(void)detailViewControllerDidClose:(CloseFriendDetailViewController *)detailViewController;
@end
```

Imports and Private Interface Setup

Now we need to move over to our `CloseFriendDetailViewController.m` file. The first thing is to add an import for the Quartz Core framework just above the `CloseFriendDetailViewController.h` import. We do this to define a border around our image using quartz core. We will also import the `UIImage+Resize.h` category to handle image resizing.

```
#import "UIImage+Resize.h"
#import <QuartzCore/QuartzCore.h>
```

We also need to create the properties that we use to interact with the Text Fields and Image View that we created in the Storyboard file.

```
@interface CloseFriendDetailViewController ()
@property (weak) IBOutlet UITextField *txtFirstName;
@property (weak) IBOutlet UITextField *txtLastName;
@property (weak) IBOutlet UITextField *txtBirthday;
@property (weak) IBOutlet UIImageView *imgFriend;

@property (strong) NSDateFormatter *dateFormatter;
@end
```

On to the Implementation

Next, we add an instance variable for the UIImagePickerController. Your @implementation line should now look like this:

```
@implementation CloseFriendDetailViewController {
    UIImagePickerController *_picker;
}
```

View Configuration Methods

We now add three methods to configure our view:

```
-(void)disableAllFields {
    [_txtFirstName setEnabled:NO];
    [_txtLastName setEnabled:NO];
    [_txtBirthday setEnabled:NO];
    for(UIGestureRecognizer *gesture in [_imgFriend gestureRecognizers]){
        [_imgFriend removeGestureRecognizer:gesture];
    }
}

-(void)enableAllFields {
    [_txtFirstName setEnabled:YES];
    [_txtLastName setEnabled:YES];
    [_txtBirthday setEnabled:YES];

    UITapGestureRecognizer *tapGesture = [[UITapGestureRecognizer alloc] initWithTarget:self
action:@selector(photoTapped:)];
    [_imgFriend addGestureRecognizer:tapGesture];
}

- (void)configureView {
    _txtFirstName.text = [_closeFriend firstName];
    _txtLastName.text = [_closeFriend lastName];
    _txtBirthday.text = [_dateFormatter stringFromDate:[_closeFriend birthday]];
    [_txtBirthday setInputView:[self setupDatePickerWithDate:[_closeFriend birthday]]];
    [_txtBirthday setInputAccessoryView:[self setupKeyboardAccessoryView]];

    _imgFriend.layer.borderColor = [UIColor darkGrayColor].CGColor;
    _imgFriend.layer.borderWidth = 2.0f;

    if([_closeFriend image] == nil)
        _imgFriend.image = [UIImage imageNamed:@"ImgNoImage"];
    else
        _imgFriend.image = [UIImage imageWithData:[_closeFriend image]];
}
```

The first two methods are used to enable and disable the editing in the view. If we are in edit mode, we will add a tap gesture to the image view that calls the photoTapped: method when the image view is tapped. When we exit edit mode, we remove the tap gesture so that tapping has no effect.

Inside the `configureView` method we start off by setting the text property of our text fields to the appropriate values. Next we set the `inputView` and `InputAccessoryView` of txtBirthday by calling two new methods that we will set up shortly. Then we use quartz core to add a border to the image view. Finally we determine whether our image is set on our object. If so, we create the `UIImage` from the `NSData` property image or we assign the image asset `ImgNoImage`.

Let's add those to input methods now:

```
-(UIDatePicker *)setupDatePickerWithDate:(NSDate *)date {
    if(date == nil)
        date = [NSDate date];

    UIDatePicker *datePicker = [[UIDatePicker alloc] init];
    [datePicker setDatePickerMode:UIDatePickerModeDate];
    [datePicker setDate:date];
    [datePicker addTarget:self action:@selector(birthdayValueChanged:)
forControlEvents:UIControlEventValueChanged];

    return datePicker;
}


-(UIView *)setupKeyboardAccessoryView {
    UIToolbar *toolbar = [[UIToolbar alloc] initWithFrame:CGRectMake(0, 0, CGRectGetWidth(self.view.
bounds), 44)];

    UIBarButtonItem *btnDone = [[UIBarButtonItem alloc] initWithTitle:@"Done"
style:UIBarButtonItemStyleBordered target:self action:@selector(btnDatePickerDonePressed:)];
    [toolbar setItems:@[btnDone]];

    return toolbar;
}
```

In the first method `setupDatePickerWithDate:` we first check to see whether we received a date. If we didn't, we set the date to today's date by calling the class method `[NSDate date];`. Next we allocate and initialize our date picker. We set the `datePickerMode` to `UIDatePickerModeDate`. This sets it so that the user is only allowed to pick a data and not a time. We then pass the date to the picker so that when the users see the date picker they are either on the current date in the birthday field or they are on the current date. Next we add a target to the `datePicker` for the event `UIControlEventValueChanged`. This causes the `birthdayValueChanged:` method to be fired every time the value of the picker is changed. Then we return this `datePicker` so that it can be used.

In the second method, we create a `UIToolbar` that is the view's width, but only 44 points high. Then we create a `UIBarButtonItem` and give it a target of `btnDatePickerDonePressed:`. Finally we call `setItems:` on the toolbar and pass it an array containing the Done button.

The `birthdayValueChanged:` method is self-explanatory and should look like this.

```
-(void)birthdayValueChanged:(UIDatePicker *)datePicker {
    _txtBirthday.text = [_dateFormatter stringFromDate:[datePicker date]];
}
```

Adding an Action Sheet for our photoTapped: Method

Next we need to add our `photoTapped:` method so that something actually happens when we tap the image.

```
-(void)photoTapped:(UIGestureRecognizer *)gesture {
    UIActionSheet *actionSheet = [[UIActionSheet alloc] initWithTitle:@"Change Photo" delegate:self
cancelButtonTitle:@"Cancel" destructiveButtonTitle:nil otherButtonTitles:@"Take Photo",@"Choose From
Library",nil];

    [actionSheet showFromTabBar:self.tabBarController.tabBar];
}
```

In this method we create a simple action sheet to ask the user if they want to take a photo with their camera or choose a photo from the photo library. We call the method `showFromTabBar:` because this view resides inside a `UITabBarController`.

Now we need to add a delegate method for the `UIActionSheet` called `actionSheet:clickedButtonAtIndex:`.

```
#pragma mark - UIActionSheetDelegate Methods
-(void)actionSheet:(UIActionSheet *)actionSheet clickedButtonAtIndex:(NSInteger)buttonIndex {
    if(_picker != nil){
        [_picker dismissViewControllerAnimated:NO completion:nil];
        _picker = nil;
    }

    switch (buttonIndex) {
        case 0: {
            _picker = [[UIImagePickerController alloc] init];
            [_picker setDelegate:self];
            [_picker setSourceType:UIImagePickerControllerSourceTypeCamera];
            [_picker setAllowsEditing:YES];

            [self presentViewController:_picker animated:YES completion:nil];
        } break;
        case 1: {
            _picker = [[UIImagePickerController alloc] init];
            [_picker setDelegate:self];
            [_picker setSourceType:UIImagePickerControllerSourceTypePhotoLibrary];
            [_picker setAllowsEditing:YES];

            [self presentViewController:_picker animated:YES completion:nil];
        } break;
        default:
            break;
    }
}
```

The method starts off by checking to see whether _picker has been allocated. If it has, then we call the method dismissViewControllerAnimated:completion: to make sure the picker is not visible. Then we assign nil to it to clear it out completely.

We use a switch statement to determine what button the user pressed. If they pressed Take Photo, then that button's index is going to be 0 and if they pressed Choose From Library, it will be 1. Inside of each case we instantiate the UIImagePickerController, set its delegate to this view controller, set the source type to UIImagePickerControllerSourceTypeCamera or UIImagePickerControllerSourceTypePhotoLibrary depending on what button they pressed, and set allows editing to YES. We then call the method presentViewController:animated:completion: on our self to display the UIImagePickerController.

Image Picker Delegate Methods

Now we need to add two UIImagePickerControllerDelegate methods.

```
#pragma mark - UIImagePickerControllerDelegate Methods
-(void)imagePickerControllerDidCancel:(UIImagePickerController *)picker {
    [self dismissViewControllerAnimated:YES completion:nil];
}

-(void)imagePickerController:(UIImagePickerController *)picker didFinishPickingMediaWithInfo:
(NSDictionary *)info {
    UIImage *image = (UIImage *)[info objectForKey:UIImagePickerControllerEditedImage];

    UIImage *resizedImage = [image resizedImage:CGSizeMake(560, 560) interpolationQuality:
kCGInterpolationHigh];
    NSData *imageData = UIImagePNGRepresentation(resizedImage);
    [_closeFriend setImage:imageData];
    [_imgFriend setImage:resizedImage];

    [self dismissViewControllerAnimated:YES completion:nil];
}
```

The first method, imagePickerControllerDidCancel: is called when the user cancels the image picker. The only thing we do here is dismiss the image picker, which brings the user back to our view.

The second method imagePickerController:didFinishPickingMediaWithInfo: is where we handle the image the user either took or selected. Because we enabled editing, the user will be creating a square image that we can access by using the constant UIImagePickerControllerEditedImage. We take that image and then resize it to 560 × 560 using the method resizeImage:interpolation Quality: that is provided in the UIImage+Resize Category on UIImage. Next we create an NSData object using the UIImagePNGRepresentation() method and pass it the resized image. We take that NSData and assign it to the image property of _closeFriend. Then we assign the image to the _imgFriend image view and dismiss our image picker.

Text Field Delegate Method

Now we need to implement one of the UITextField delegate methods called textFieldShouldReturn:. You have already done this before so it should be familiar.

```
#pragma mark - UITextFieldDelegate Methods
-(BOOL)textFieldShouldReturn:(UITextField *)textField {
    if([textField isEqual:_txtFirstName]){
        [_txtLastName becomeFirstResponder];
    } else if([textField isEqual:_txtLastName]){
        [_txtBirthday becomeFirstResponder];
    }

    return YES;
}
```

Here we check the text field and move to the next text field similar to what we have done in the past.

Bar Button Methods

Now we add some Bar Button methods:

```
#pragma mark - Bar Button Methods
-(void)btnEditPressed:(id)sender {
    [self enableAllFields];
    UIBarButtonItem *doneButton = [[UIBarButtonItem alloc] initWithTitle:@"Done"
style:UIBarButtonItemStyleDone target:self action:@selector(btnDonePressed:)];
    [self.navigationItem setRightBarButtonItem:doneButton animated:YES];

    [self.navigationItem setLeftBarButtonItem:nil animated:YES];
}

-(void)btnDonePressed:(id)sender {
    [self disableAllFields];

    [_closeFriend setFirstName:_txtFirstName.text];
    [_closeFriend setLastName:_txtLastName.text];
    [_closeFriend setBirthday:[_dateFormatter dateFromString:_txtBirthday.text]];

    UIBarButtonItem *editButton = [[UIBarButtonItem alloc] initWithTitle:@"Edit"
style:UIBarButtonItemStyleBordered target:self action:@selector(btnEditPressed:)];
    [self.navigationItem setRightBarButtonItem:editButton animated:YES];

    UIBarButtonItem *backButton = [[UIBarButtonItem alloc] initWithTitle:@"Back"
style:UIBarButtonItemStyleBordered target:self action:@selector(btnBackPressed:)];
    [self.navigationItem setLeftBarButtonItem:backButton animated:YES];
}
```

```
-(void)btnBackPressed:(id)sender {
    NSError *error = nil;
    if(![[AppDelegate managedObjectContext] save:&error]){
        NSLog(@"There was an error saving date - %@",error.localizedDescription);
        [[[UIAlertView alloc] initWithTitle:@"Error" message:[NSString stringWithFormat:@"There
was an error saving data - %@",error.localizedDescription] delegate:nil cancelButtonTitle:@"OK"
otherButtonTitles:nil] show];
    } else {
        [_delegate detailViewControllerDidClose:self];
    }
}

-(void)btnDatePickerDonePressed:(id)sender {
    static NSDateFormatter *dateFormatter = nil;
    if (dateFormatter == nil) {
        dateFormatter = [[NSDateFormatter alloc] init];
        [dateFormatter setDateStyle:NSDateFormatterMediumStyle];
    }

    UIDatePicker *datePicker = (UIDatePicker *)_txtBirthday.inputView;
    _txtBirthday.text = [dateFormatter stringFromDate:datePicker.date];
    [_txtBirthday resignFirstResponder];
}
```

The first method btnEditPressed: enables all the fields for editing by calling our enableAllFields method. Then we create a UIBarButtonItem titled "Done" and give it an action of btnDonePressed:. We replace the right Bar Button item with our Done button and remove the left Bar Button item. Removing the left Bar Button item makes sure that the user is not in an edit mode when they return to the collection view.

The second method is btnDonePressed:. We disable all the fields by calling our disableAllFields method. Then we set up the Bar Buttons back to their original state by creating an editButton and a Back button, adding those to our navigation item.

The third method is btnBackPressed: and we simply perform a save on our managed object context. If it fails, we show an alert message and use NSLog to log the message to console for debugging. If all is well, then we call our delegate method detailViewControllerDidClose: and pass our self as the parameter.

Wrapping Up Our View Controller Code

The last thing we need to do is set up our viewDidLoad:

```
- (void)viewDidLoad
{
    [super viewDidLoad];

    _dateFormatter = [[NSDateFormatter alloc] init];
    [_dateFormatter setDateStyle:NSDateFormatterMediumStyle];
```

```
    UIBarButtonItem *editButton = [[UIBarButtonItem alloc] initWithTitle:@"Edit"
style:UIBarButtonItemStyleBordered target:self action:@selector(btnEditPressed:)];
    [self.navigationItem setRightBarButtonItem:editButton];

    UIBarButtonItem *backButton = [[UIBarButtonItem alloc] initWithTitle:@"Back"
style:UIBarButtonItemStyleBordered target:self action:@selector(btnBackPressed:)];
    [self.navigationItem setLeftBarButtonItem:backButton];
    [self.navigationItem setHidesBackButton:YES];

    [self configureView];
    [self disableAllFields];

    if(_shouldStartEditing) {
        [self btnEditPressed:nil];
        [_txtFirstName becomeFirstResponder];
    }
}
}
```

This should be self-explanatory by now. We initialize our NSDateFormatter and set its dateStyle to NSDateFormatterMediumStyle. We create our Bar Buttons and assign them accordingly. We then call our configure view that sets our image border and applies our default image. We disable all the fields so that we aren't in edit mode. Then we check to see whether we shouldStartEditing and if so, we simulate the Edit button being pressed by calling btnEditPressed:. Finally, we set the first text field to become the first responder so that it becomes selected and the keyboard shows.

Because we have now finished up with the CloseFriendDetailViewController we need to go back to the CloseFriendsTableViewController.h and make a few changes. First we need to add the import statement for our CloseFriendDetailViewController.h file just above the UIKit import.

```
#import "CloseFriendDetailViewController.h"
```

The last thing we need to do is subscribe to the CloseFriendDetailViewControllerDelegate protocol. The interface should now look like this:

```
@interface CloseFriendsTableViewController : UITableViewController
<CloseFriendDetailViewControllerDelegate>
```

Moving over to the CloseFriendsTableViewController.m file we need to add this delegate method:

```
#pragma mark - CloseFriendDetailViewControllerDelegate Methods
-(void)detailViewControllerDidClose:(CloseFriendDetailViewController *)detailViewController {
    [self.navigationController popToRootViewControllerAnimated:YES];

    [self.tableView reloadData];
}
```

This simply removes the CloseFriendDetailViewController by popping to the CloseFriendsTableViewController and reloads our tableview.

Storyboard Modifications

The final thing we need to do is to set up our Storyboard to interact with these class files.

1. Select the `UITableViewController` in the Storyboard and set its class to `CloseFriendsTableViewController`.

2. Ctrl-drag from the Add Button to the `TableViewController` and select `btnAddPressed:` from the pop-up.

3. Select the `UIViewController` in the Storyboard and set its class to `CloseFriendDetailViewController`.

4. In the Connections Inspector, drag a connection for `imgFriend`, `txtBirthday`, `txtFirstName`, and `txtLastName` to the appropriate object in the view.

5. Next, Ctrl-drag from each of the text fields to the `CloseFriendDetailViewController` object and select delegate underneath Outlets in the popup.

Go ahead and build and run the app. You should be able to add new Close Friends and delete them if you wish. You can select an image in the Detail view and it will show up in that view. All this data is being saved locally. Now I will show you how quick and easy it is to integrate iCloud with Core Data.

Adding iCloud to Core Data

Because we are going to add iCloud support we need to tell our persistent store that it will be iCloud enabled. We do this is by creating an `NSDictionary` with optional parameters and passing that to the `addPersistentStoreWithType:configuration:URL:options:error` method. We do this in our Application Delegate, which is where all our Core Data Stack code is. Find the `persistentStoreCoordinator` method in `CTAppDelegate.m` and change it to this:

```
- (NSPersistentStoreCoordinator *)persistentStoreCoordinator
{
    if (_persistentStoreCoordinator != nil) {
        return _persistentStoreCoordinator;
    }

    NSURL *storeURL = [[self applicationDocumentsDirectory] URLByAppendingPathComponent:
@"iCloudTestApp.sqlite"];

    NSError *error = nil;
    _persistentStoreCoordinator = [[NSPersistentStoreCoordinator alloc] initWithManagedObjectModel:
[self managedObjectModel]];

    NSDictionary *options = @{NSPersistentStoreUbiquitousContentNameKey:@"Store"};

    if (![_persistentStoreCoordinator addPersistentStoreWithType:NSSQLiteStoreType configuration:nil
URL:storeURL options:options error:&error]) {
```

```
        NSLog(@"Unresolved error %@, %@", error, [error userInfo]);
        abort();
    }

    return _persistentStoreCoordinator;
}
```

As you can see, we added an options dictionary. We use the key NSPersistentStoreUbiquitousContentNameKey and give it a value of Store. We then pass that options object as the option parameter in the addPersistentStoreWithType:configuration:URL:options: error: method. I know it may sound simple, but you have just enabled iCloud support. But we aren't done setting up our app to handle the notifications I mentioned earlier. Let's add our self as an observer to those by modifying the method managedObjectContext.

```
- (NSManagedObjectContext *)managedObjectContext
{
    if (_managedObjectContext != nil) {
        return _managedObjectContext;
    }

    NSPersistentStoreCoordinator *coordinator = [self persistentStoreCoordinator];
    if (coordinator != nil) {
        _managedObjectContext = [[NSManagedObjectContext alloc] init];
        [_managedObjectContext setPersistentStoreCoordinator:coordinator];

        [[NSNotificationCenter defaultCenter] addObserver:self selector:@selector(persiste
ntStoreDidImportContent:) name:NSPersistentStoreDidImportUbiquitousContentChangesNotification
object:coordinator];
        [[NSNotificationCenter defaultCenter] addObserver:self selector:@selector
(persistentStoresWillChange:) name:NSPersistentStoreCoordinatorStoresWillChangeNotification
object:coordinator];
        [[NSNotificationCenter defaultCenter] addObserver:self selector:@selector(persistent
StoresDidChange:) name:NSPersistentStoreCoordinatorStoresDidChangeNotification object:coordinator];
    }
    return _managedObjectContext;
}
```

The only lines we added here are the three notifications. We are now listening for NSPersistentStoreDidImportUbiquitousContentChangesNotification, NSPersistentStoreCoordinatoreStoresWillChangeNotification, and NSPersistenLStoreCoordinatorStoresDidChangeNotification. Now we need to write the three selectors we referenced.

```
#pragma mark - iCloud Core Data Notification Methods
-(void)persistentStoresWillChange:(NSNotification *)notification {
    if([_managedObjectContext hasChanges]){
```

```
        NSError *error = nil;
        if(![_managedObjectContext save:&error]){
            NSLog(@"Error while trying to save data before store will change - %@",error.
localizedDescription);
        }
    }

    [_managedObjectContext reset];
}

-(void)persistentStoresDidChange:(NSNotification *)notification {
    [[NSNotificationCenter defaultCenter] postNotificationName:@"PERSISTENT_STORE_CHANGED"
object:nil];
}

-(void)persistentStoreDidImportContent:(NSNotification *)notification {
    [_managedObjectContext mergeChangesFromContextDidSaveNotification:notification];

    [[NSNotificationCenter defaultCenter] postNotificationName:@"PERSISTENT_STORE_UPDATED"
object:nil];
}
```

In the first method we are notified that the store will change. Because we still have access to the store, we first check to see whether we have changes by calling [_managedObjectContext hasChanges];. If we do, then we try to save. If there is an error we use NSLog to log it for debugging. Once saved, we call reset on our managedObjectContext to set it back to its base state.

In the second method, we post a notification to let our app know that we are using a new persistent store. We will use this in just a little bit to update our UI.

In the final method we call the method mergeChangesFromContextDidSaveNotification: on our managed object context and pass it the notification. This method handles the merging of changes received from iCloud and will refresh, add, and/or remove any objects it needs to from the current context. Finally, we post a notification letting our app know that the store has been updated in case we need to do anything at that time.

Now let's move over to our CloseFriendsTableViewController.m file and add it as an observer for those notifications. The viewDidLoad method should now look like this:

```
- (void)viewDidLoad
{
    [super viewDidLoad];

    [self loadCloseFriends];
    [[NSNotificationCenter defaultCenter] addObserver:self selector:@selector(persistentStoreUpdated:)
name:@"PERSISTENT_STORE_UPDATED" object:nil];
    [[NSNotificationCenter defaultCenter] addObserver:self selector:@selector(persistentStoreChanged:)
name:@"PERSISTENT_STORE_CHANGED" object:nil];
}
```

We also override the dealloc method to remove ourselves as an observer.

```
-(void)dealloc {
    [[NSNotificationCenter defaultCenter] removeObserver:self];
}
```

Now we need to write the persistentStoreUpdated: and persistentStoreChanged: methods.

```
-(void)persistentStoreUpdated:(NSNotification *)notification {
    [self loadCloseFriends];
    [self.tableView reloadData];
}
```

```
-(void)persistentStoreChanged:(NSNotificationCenter *)notification {
    [self loadCloseFriends];
    [self.tableView reloadData];
}
```

As you can see we are just reloading our _closeFriends array and reloading our table view. This keeps the data we see fresh and removes the possibility that it might be stale.

We have one more change to make and that is in the CloseFriendDetailViewController.m file. In this file we will override the viewWillAppear: and viewDidDisappear: methods.

```
-(void)viewWillAppear:(BOOL)animated {
    [super viewWillAppear:animated];

    [[NSNotificationCenter defaultCenter] addObserver:self selector:@selector(persistentStoreChanged:)
name:@"PERSISTENT_STORE_CHANGED" object:nil];
    [[NSNotificationCenter defaultCenter] addObserver:self selector:@selector(persistentStoreUpdated:)
name:@"PERSISTENT_STORE_UPDATED" object:nil];
}
```

```
-(void)viewDidDisappear:(BOOL)animated {
    [super viewDidDisappear:animated];

    [[NSNotificationCenter defaultCenter] removeObserver:self];
}
```

We use the viewWillAppear: and viewDidDisappear: methods in this instance because we only care about these changes if the view is showing. We already know that if we are pushing to this view we have a current valid object.

Now let's write these two methods and wrap up.

```
-(void)persistentStoreChanged:(NSNotification *)notification {
    [_delegate detailViewControllerDidClose:self];
}
```

```
-(void)persistentStoreUpdated:(NSNotification *)notification {
    if(_closeFriend == nil)
        [_delegate detailViewControllerDidClose:self];
    else
        [self configureView];
}
```

In the first method we simply call our delegate method. This will ultimately pop this view controller off the stack.

In the second method we check to see whether our managed object has been deleted by iCloud. If it has, we call our delegate method. If it has not, we update our view by calling our configureView method.

That's it. You are now ready to take your friendly app completely to the cloud. Add a few close friends and then delete the app. Watch them return almost instantly. Try logging in with a different iCloud account to see how the application reacts to the account change.

Summary

In this chapter we learned the basics of integrating iCloud with Core Data. We learned several of Core Data's newer features including automatic validation of property values and schema migration. Remember, you can learn more about these features by visiting http://developer.apple.com. We also discussed the Fallback Store and how Apple has recently assumed responsibility of it so that developers no longer need to manage multiple stores, and how this has led to an asynchronous process versus the previous synchronous one.

Finally, we added Close Friends to our Friend app, allowing us to view birthdays of our friends. We then added iCloud to Core Data, completing our first app integrated with iCloud!

Chapter 7

Testing and App Submission

After you have finished coding your iCloud application, substantial testing will be necessary. This doesn't simply ensure that your app is bug-free and looks nice, but that iCloud is working with your app exactly the way you intend. Apple has once again given developers great tools to use with the introduction of iOS 7. These tools give developers easier access to the API and the ability to test the connections in real-time. Once you are confident that the app is thoroughly tested and debugged, we'll discuss the submission of your app to the App Store.

New Debugging in Xcode

There are new tools you need to use to help you prepare your application for deployment. Figure 7-1 shows that iCloud is now included in Xcode 5. Substantial improvements have been made to Xcode for this version, especially surrounding debugging.

Figure 7-1. Xcode 5 now has an iCloud panel for real time testing

You can now see the amount of storage space used and space available, what is uploading or downloading, and the UIDocuments you have stored for the current user.

The file transfer graph is shown in Figure 7-2. This tool becomes invaluable in testing an iCloud account by letting you see exactly what is happening and when it happens.

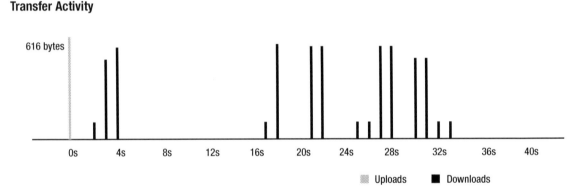

Figure 7-2. The real-time graph of uploads and downloads in the Xcode iCloud Debugger

Security Considerations

Guard the credentials to your Apple developer accounts. This is vitally important. Not only should you keep any developer accounts safeguarded, but your account credentials should be complex enough to prevent someone from cracking them with brute force. If someone has access to your developer accounts, it potentially gives them the ability to release an app with the same Bundle Seed ID. Because Apple uses the Bundle Seed ID to constrain access to user data in iCloud between different organizations, if an attacker were to issue a provisioning profile with your Team ID, it would allow them to access the user's iCloud containers and ferry that information back to themselves.

Connectivity Testing

After coding your initial UX, it is best practice to test the application on several devices and in several scenarios. This not only helps you find bugs in your app or in the iCloud coding, but also gives you a better picture of the user experience, as well as whether files are being stored or transferred in the best possible way. Start easy, then work your way into more complex scenarios. Ensure your devices and your apps on the devices are connected to iCloud before getting started.

As shown in Figure 7-3, you can launch the iOS Simulator and test the iCloud account. If you are using devices, go through the following steps for device testing.

Figure 7-3. Now in iOS 7, your iOS simulator supports iCloud accounts

Begin by making a change to an iCloud document on one device, and be sure it appears on another. Using Apple's Calendar app as an example, if while I'm on my iPhone I add an event to a specific day on the calendar, that information should be pushed to the Calendar app on my iPad and my MacBook as well. Check the time it took to get there and what data was saved in which locations. Walk through the app several times with each device. Your goal is to make the app stop working properly so you can catch whatever's wrong before anyone else.

Once your app gets out into the hands of the public, you'll find that actual continuous use of your iCloud-enabled app can result in many different issues of conflict. While this is inescapable, you could be including unnecessary conflicts in your app that are easily avoidable. For example, in an app that saves edits and updates to a document, the document should not be saved unless an edit was actually made.

Let's say you create a photo-editing app that lets you edit several photos at a time. If someone makes several edits to their photos while on their iPhone, those edits should appear on their other devices. However, if that person decides to later scroll through to the end of those photos on their iPad, but never actually makes any changes to the photos, should the simple fact that the user scrolled be saved and pushed to other devices? When the user opens the photos on the MacBook Pro, should they be scrolled to the end as they were on their iPad? Most likely the answer is no. This is an unhelpful and trivial save that will consume the user's network bandwidth and their device's battery.

Editing a Document on Multiple Devices

Earlier I talked about testing different devices and editing documents at the same time. Here is a walkthrough of how to do that, only we'll take it a step further and test while one of the devices is offline.

1. Connect two devices that can run your app to a single iCloud account.

2. Open a document in your app on both devices so that they are running at the same time.

3. On one of the devices, turn on Airplane mode, and then edit the document.

4. Now, edit the document on the other device, which is left online.

5. Finally, turn off Airplane mode on the first device, so that both devices are online. On each device you can now check whether the conflict resolution behavior acted as you intended.

You can then run the same test, only before editing the documents, put both devices in Airplane mode. You can play with this by turning off Airplane mode on one first, and then the other, or attempting it at the same time. Again, check whether the conflict resolution that took place is what you intended.

Testing Forward and Backward Compatibility

Once you have multiple versions of your app, you can test the forward and backward compatibility of your document format.

1. Install the oldest supported version of your app on one device, and then install the newest version on the second device.

2. On each device you will need to create a document, before allowing enough time to elapse so that the document from each device appears on the other one.

3. Open the documents on the devices that were not originally used to create the document and check for any issues that occur. Depending on your app, you may be able to make changes to a single document on different devices that host different versions of your app.

4. Record what takes place when you do these tests to ensure that it works according to your intentions.

Testing Saves to iCloud

As you know, iCloud isn't just for automatically pushing edits in documents to other devices. iCloud allows you to store items directly to their servers using an online management system.

1. One way to test your document management with iCloud is to first save a document to iCloud.

2. Then, open that document on two separate devices.

3. On the first device delete the document or simply rename it.

4. Check the document on the second device to ensure that it behaves as you intend.

When you are developing an app with iCloud, it is possible for data in the app's ubiquity container to become inconsistent, which can cause your app to behave inconsistently as well. Maybe some of the code that you know was working previously is no longer working. A solution to this problem is to simply start fresh, which can be done by emptying your app's ubiquity container. This can be done on either an iOS device or on a Mac.

Emptying the Ubiquity Container

If you want to empty the ubiquity container for your app using an iOS device, you will need to delete each instance of your app on each device.

1. Navigate to Settings ➤ iCloud ➤ Storage & Backup ➤ Manage Storage

2. Select your app's name on the screen. If it is not shown in the Documents and Data group, then tap Show All.

3. On the app's storage information screen, tap Edit.

4. Select Delete All.

5. An alert will appear asking you to confirm this deletion. Tap on Confirm to finish this process.

After doing this, wait a short time to be sure that your ubiquity container's contents are deleted on all the devices attached to your iCloud account. The time it takes may depend on the amount of data the container was holding. To see whether the ubiquity container has been emptied on a Mac, use the Finder. Once each instance has been deleted, reinstall the app on each device.

To empty the ubiquity container for your application using a Mac, you will also need to delete each instance of the app on each device:

1. In System Preferences, open iCloud preferences and click Manage.

2. Locate your app in the Manage Storage dialog that appears and click on it.

3. Then click Delete All.

4. An alert will appear asking you to confirm this deletion. Click on Confirm to finish this process.

Again, wait to confirm that the ubiquity container's contents have been deleted on all devices attached to the iCloud account and reinstall the app on each device.

Other Tests

Now, test the application on one device while the others are off. When you turn on the device later, check whether the update takes place, how long it took, and whether anything is different from the previous test. If all is well in these scenarios, begin testing what happens when you make multiple changes to the same document at the same time while on separate devices. Which versions of the documents take precedent? Do the documents integrate with one another, or does a single version become the new master copy? Check whether different versions appear on different devices. While there are certainly default or common ways these questions get answered, the most important thing is whether, after testing these aspects of how iCloud integrates with your app, the current way files are transferred, changed, and saved makes the most sense for your application.

There are a million ways to test your app in conjunction with iCloud: Check the locations where specific files and critical data are being stored. Test the amount of data being sent, received, and stored. Test with different devices in Airplane mode. Test the time on push notifications. You can test on a train, in a bus, on a plane! You get the picture. It is to be expected that you'll find some bugs, storage issues, UX slips, or other problems when first testing an application. Go back, tweak the code, then test some more.

Be sure your device is configured for iCloud and that all the devices you are testing on are properly provisioned for iCloud. This includes your device's provisioning profile and the app ID. Also, make sure the entitlement requests are correct. If your app does not have the correct entitlement requests in place within your Xcode project, your app will not have access to its ubiquity containers or key-value storage.

Provisioning and Entitlements

A Development Provisioning Profile contains a set of Unique Device Identifiers (commonly called UDIDs), iPhone Development Certificates, and an App ID. These define the devices that are allowed to run your application, and the location of your iCloud storage. All the storage space that your application uses will be allocated by whatever team you happen to be on.

Uniquely tying developers and devices to an authorized iPhone Development Team, provisioning profiles are basically a collection of entities that enables a device to be used for testing. Because of this, a provisioning profile needs to be installed on *each* device on which you want to run your application's code. To review a walkthrough of provisioning profile creation, see Chapter 4.

While provisioning profiles define the devices that can run your app, entitlements are the things that allow your application to access the iCloud container at runtime. You will need to have both of these in place before you begin your testing. An important part of the iOS security framework, entitlements also allow iCloud to access your ubiquity container in a safe manner.

Renewing Expired Provisioning Profiles

As an iOS developer, you will continually find yourself at the Apple iPhone Provisioning Portal. This is because you will need to renew various certificates now and again, such as developer certificates, various Apple Push Notification certificates, and your Provisioning profiles. The fact that these will all expire at different times means you need to do this relatively frequently.

Development provisioning profiles will usually expire every three months or so even if you haven't submitted your application to the App Store, so you will have to renew these profiles. You will receive warning messages for several weeks before it expires, so there is little worry about missing this deadline. If, however, you do allow the profile to expire, the application will not launch on the device. Furthermore, if you attempt to build and install the application from Xcode, you will get an error that reads:

```
Code Sign error: Provisioning profile 'App-name' has expired
```

Within the device, you can also see in advance when profiles will expire. Under Settings ➤ General ➤ Profiles, you will see a list of all the profiles installed on the device, as well as the date it will expire. Clicking on it will give you further information, like the day it was created, and will allow you to remove the profile if you desire.

To renew a profile, visit the iPhone Provisioning Portal. On the Profiles page, you will see a profile with the status of Expired, along with a Renew button under Actions.

Clicking Renew changes the status of the profile to Pending. Refresh the page, and it should now have the status as Active. Download and save it. After you have done this, the provisioning profile needs to be installed. In the Xcode Organizer window, drag the new profile onto the Provisioning Profiles page. Be sure to delete the old, expired profile, which should now have a red cross next to it in the profile list.

You should now be able to install the app on the device without error. Two things to look out for however are to make sure the correct profile is being used, and that you have only one provisioning profile installed for your single application. If you do not, you may see the error:

```
Error launching remote program: security policy error.
```

If this is the case, simply go onto your device and delete the old profile as described previously. If other problems persist, it may be worth doing a complete clean and rebuild. Go to Product ➤ Clean in the Xcode menu to clean your build. If this does not resolve your problem you can clean your build folder by selecting the Product menu and pressing the option key on your keyboard. This will change the Clean option to the Clean Build Folder option. Select it and once it completes, just rebuild your project. Building after preforming a clean will take a little longer than a standard build.

App Submission and Approval

Compared to every other app deployment, iOS makes you jump through the most hoops. And while this can be somewhat annoying, it's a process that is secure, and ensures that apps that get posted are of a certain level of quality that users have come to expect from iOS apps. There are quality controls in place that ensure apps don't have glaring bugs or crashes, contain unacceptable content, and that the app really is what you tell Apple it is. This process can take up to two weeks, and can be somewhat maddening, because it's unclear the exact day and time the app will get published. If you're planning a launch party, you'll need to plan it far enough in advance to ensure the app is posted, but know that it's likely to have already been there for some time before the party takes place.

In the event that something catastrophic does happen to delay your app submission you can request an expedited review. This should never be used as common practice, but Apple does realize that sometimes things just happen. Apple also notifies you that all expedite requests are granted on a limited basis, and they cannot guarantee that every request will be approved. To do this you would need to log into your developer account and then select "App Store Resource Center" located in the Resources menu on the Footer of the page. On the App Store Resource Center page you should see a section for Contact Us. There will be a link in that section titled "Request an Expedited App Review." Select that link and fill out all required fields.

While one can assume memory leaks are one of the primary things Apple is looking out for, there are plenty of applications on the store that have memory leaks or other performance issues. The only place where a memory leak causes a problem during review is when that memory leak gets so bad that the application crashes when the reviewer is testing it. If your application crashes at any point during the review process, it will be rejected.

Beyond that, Apple has a checklist of user interface elements that they check for proper usage, such as no persistent selections on table view rows. If your application deviates significantly from the Human Interface Guidelines when using these standard UI elements, your app may get rejected; otherwise, it should be a breeze getting approval after all the testing is complete.

Summary

In this chapter, we discussed testing your application and its submission to the App Store. Testing has become a smoother process with Xcode's new tools, but manually testing the application in a wide variety of scenarios is still necessary to ensure a complete and finished product. Always remember to guard the credentials to your Apple developer accounts. Not everyone in the world is as honest as you. Finally, despite deployment to the App Store being as involved as it is, it actually allows you peace of mind, knowing that Apple only gives their approval to finished apps. You don't want to put something out that is of low quality. So sit back, relax, and be patient, knowing that your app will be approved and submitted when it is ready.

Congratulations on creating your first app with iCloud integration!

Index

▓ V, W, X, Y, Z

Get the eBook for only $10!

Now you can take the weightless companion with you anywhere, anytime. Your purchase of this book entitles you to 3 electronic versions for only $10.

This Apress title will prove so indispensible that you'll want to carry it with you everywhere, which is why we are offering the eBook in 3 formats for only $10 if you have already purchased the print book.

Convenient and fully searchable, the PDF version enables you to easily find and copy code—or perform examples by quickly toggling between instructions and applications. The MOBI format is ideal for your Kindle, while the ePUB can be utilized on a variety of mobile devices.

Go to www.apress.com/promo/tendollars to purchase your companion eBook.